Eight Verses
for Training the Mind

Eight Verses
for Training the Mind

An Oral Teaching
by
Geshe Sonam Rinchen

Translated and Edited
by
Ruth Sonam

Snow Lion Publications
Ithaca, New York

Snow Lion Publications
P.O. Box 6483
Ithaca, New York 14851 USA
607-273-8519
www.snowlionpub.com

First edition USA 2001

ISBN 1-55939-165-0

Printed in USA on acid-free, recycled paper.

Library of Congress Cataloging-in-Publication Data
Sonam Rinchen, 1933–
Eight verses for training the mind : an oral teaching / by Geshe Sonam
    Rinchen ; translated and edited by Ruth Sonam.
    p. cm.
Based on Langri Tangpa's Blo sbyoṅ tshig brgyad ma.
ISBN 1-55939-165-0 (alk. paper)
1. Langri Tangpa, 1054–1123. Blo sbyoṅ tshig brgyad ma. 2. Spiritual life—
Bka'-gdams-pa (Sect) 3. Bka'-gdams-pa (Sect)—Doctrines. I. Sonam, Ruth,
1943– II. Langri Tangpa, 1054–1123. Blo sbyoṅ tshig brgyad ma. English.
BQ7670.6.L34 S66 2001
294.3'420423—dc21
                                                                      2001003404

Contents

Acknowledgment

I would like to thank my editor Susan Kyser.

Chapter One

The Authenticity of the Teaching

These eight verses for training one's mind belong to a special category of teachings unique to the Great Vehicle.[1] The mind to be tamed and trained is, of course, our own, and the training consists of ridding ourselves of negative mental states and fostering and developing constructive ones.[2] All negative thoughts and feelings, which cause us so much trouble and suffering, stem from our self-concern and our misconceptions. To overcome self-concern we need to develop heartfelt concern for others, the highest expression of which is the spirit of enlightenment.[3] To rid ourselves of misconceptions, which distort our perception of how things exist, we need the correct understanding of reality supported by this spirit of enlightenment.

It is essential to approach the teachings of the Great Vehicle in the right way. If we are only concerned with gaining respect, reward and a good reputation, the outcome of our efforts will be limited to the well-being of this life, and what we do will not be a true practice of the Buddha's teachings. If we hope to gain a good rebirth in favorable conditions as a human or celestial being, what we do to accomplish this constitutes authentic practice of the Buddha's teachings but the result will necessarily be limited by the narrowness of our aspiration.

When we acknowledge the disadvantages of cyclic existence and are intent on liberation from the suffering it entails, our practice acts as a cause for our own peace but remains restricted to our own personal benefit. The special attitudes needed when we turn to the Mahayana teachings are concern for the ultimate happiness of all living beings and the intention to become enlightened in order to achieve that end.

As the Tibetan master Dromtönpa[4] lay dying, his disciple Geshe Potowa[5] cradled his spiritual master's head in his lap. Feeling quite lost and overwhelmed by grief, his tears fell on Dromtönpa, who looked up at him and told him not to grieve but to take kindheartedness as his quintessential practice. Jowo Lek,[6] who was present in the room, asked what this meant, and Dromtönpa replied that it meant keeping the spirit of enlightenment in one's heart at all times. For some moments Potowa felt comforted by this but then he remembered that to develop the spirit of enlightenment one needs the guidance of a properly qualified spiritual teacher, and his grief returned.

While the great Indian master Atisha,[7] Dromtönpa's own main spiritual teacher, was still alive, it was his custom, no matter where he traveled, to remind people in a very direct way to be kindhearted. Je Tsongkhapa[8] reiterates the importance of this by saying that it is not enough for the teaching to belong to the Great Vehicle—the practitioner also must belong to the Great Vehicle. He or she should have the spirit of enlightenment or at least have a strong wish to develop it.

Without the spirit of enlightenment what we do can never become a Mahayana practice, whereas with it even the most mundane activities become true practices of the Great Vehicle. Once the spirit of enlightenment has become spontaneous and constantly present in us, the effect is inconceivably powerful, but even if we still have to make repeated effort to arouse it, it is worth doing so because through it the positive actions we perform become a cause for complete enlightenment. Like a precious elixir, it can turn our normal activities into gold.

On one occasion when Atisha had been in Tibet for some time, he met an Indian scholar and the two spent the evening talking about the latest events in India. The scholar mentioned that a practitioner of the Hevajra tantra[9] had attained the stage of Stream Enterer.[10] Atisha found this piece of news astonishing. The practice of tantra is an aspect of the Great Vehicle and is normally undertaken with the intention of attaining complete enlightenment as swiftly as possible for the sake of others. The reason why this practitioner had attained the state of a Stream Enterer and become an exalted being of the Hearer Vehicle was because he had engaged in the practice of Hevajra with the motivation to attain personal liberation from cyclic existence and not with the spirit of enlightenment. The scholar remarked that had he practiced without even this motivation, he would probably have gone straight into a bad rebirth.

From all this we see how important it is to train our mind because the motivation with which we practice determines the outcome. The Kadampa masters considered the spirit of enlightenment as the fulcrum for practice and they viewed the insights of the initial and intermediate levels[11] as the essential preparations for developing the spirit of enlightenment. The practices of the highest level, such as the six perfections[12] and the practice of tantra, were for them ways of strengthening and enhancing that spirit of enlightenment. This shows clearly that tantra is integral to the stages of the path to enlightenment and is not to be regarded as something separate. Without both the conventional and ultimate forms of the spirit of enlightenment[13] the practice of tantra cannot be effective.

The teachings for training one's mind combine both the extensive and profound aspects of practice, which have their source in the Buddha's Perfection of Wisdom sutras[14] and in the *Avatamsaka Sutra*.[15] The extensive aspect, which is mainly concerned with the activities of Bodhisattvas, was passed from Maitreya[16] to Asanga[17] and eventually reached Atisha. The profound aspect, to do with the understanding of reality, reached Atisha through Manjushri,[18] Nagarjuna[19] and other great Indian masters. The teachings belonging to the inspiring practice lineage,[20] particularly those about equalizing and exchanging self and others, came to Atisha through Manjushri, Shantideva[21] and Dharmakirti of the Golden Isles.[22] The *Eight Verses for Training the Mind* mainly draws on this particular aspect of the teachings.

When Atisha was already a great scholar in sutra and tantra, a series of experiences convinced him that developing the spirit of enlightenment was essential if he wished to gain enlightenment. On one occasion, when he was circumambulating the great stupa in Bodhgaya,[23] he saw two women hovering in the sky before him. As he watched, the younger paid homage to the older one and asked her what was most important if one wished to attain enlightenment, to which the older one replied that it was the spirit of enlightenment. Inside the stupa he saw the smaller statues bowing to the bigger ones and heard the bigger ones give the same answer to this question.

Inspired by this, he eventually made the perilous thirteen-month sea journey to Indonesia with a number of his students to meet Dharmakirti of the Golden Isles, who at that time was said to possess the fullest instructions for developing the spirit of enlightenment. With lavish gifts he requested the master to give him complete teachings on how to do this. Dharmakirti inquired whether he thought he could develop great love and compassion and whether he was prepared to stay for twelve years. Atisha replied in the affirmative to both of these questions, and so his apprenticeship began.

He remained with this master for twelve years, received the entire instructions from him and developed the spirit of enlightenment by putting the instructions into practice. When the time came for him to leave, his master gave him a small statue of the Buddha that he had kept by him since he was a child. In this way he made Atisha his spiritual heir and predicted that Atisha would one day teach in a snowy northern land.

Atisha fulfilled this prediction by accepting the invitation to teach in Tibet. Although he had many disciples in India, Nepal and Tibet, his closest disciple and true spiritual son was Dromtön Gyelway Jungnay, regarding whom Arya Tara[24] had made a prophecy to Atisha.

While he was in Tibet, Atisha taught mainly the importance of taking sincere refuge in the Three Jewels and how this should be done, and the connection between actions and their effects. Because of this he became known as the "Refuge Lama" and the "Karma Lama." When he heard about these nicknames he was pleased and not at all offended. To Dromtönpa he taught the complete stages of the path to enlightenment. One day Dromtönpa asked why he was the only one to have received this teaching and Atisha told him that he had found no one else who was ready for it. By bestowing this teaching on him, Atisha, in turn, made Dromtönpa his spiritual heir.

After Atisha's death, his relics were taken to Reting, where a stupa was constructed to house them. A monastery was built there from which the Kadampa teachings spread. Much later Je Tsongkhapa praised Dromtönpa for "illuminating the good path."

Dromtönpa's spiritual heirs were the "three Kadampa brothers," Geshe Potowa, Geshe Chengawa and Geshe Pülchungwa.[25] The foremost of these was Geshe Potowa, who was both a great teacher and a great practitioner. In his teaching he combined the mind-training tradition that came from Dharmakirti of the Golden Isles with what became known as the six Kadampa texts: the *Bodhisattva Stages* by Asanga, the *Ornament for the Mahayana Sutras* by Maitreya, the *Stories of the Buddha's Past Lives* by Aryashura, *The Compendium*, a collection of statements by the Buddha, Shantideva's *Compendium of Training* and his *Way of the Bodhisattva*.[26]

It is important to understand that the teaching contained in the *Eight Verses for Training the Mind* is not something thought up by Tibetans. The Tibetan form of Buddhism has often erroneously been referred to as "Lamaism," as if it were something quite different from Indian Buddhism. This is a serious mistake. Buddhism was adopted so completely by Tibetans that it became their own, and although some of the outer forms may have been influenced by Tibetan culture, the inner essence has remained unchanged. Through the work of the great translators, a vast corpus of Buddhist literature was translated into Tibetan. The faithfulness of these translations is apparent when they are compared to texts or fragments of texts which are still extant in Sanskrit.

It became possible for Tibetans to study and practice the Buddha's teaching without the need to learn Sanskrit because the Tibetan translators formulated a language capable of expressing the most subtle philosophical concepts. This gives us food for thought. How wonderful it would be if similar work could be done now to translate books explaining the great discoveries made in the Western world into Tibetan, so that Tibetans could learn about these things in their own language.

Geshe Potowa is said to have had more than two thousand students and eight close disciples. Preeminent among these disciples were Geshe Langritangpa Dorje Senge[27] and Geshe Sharawa,[28] who were compared to the sun and the moon. Just like his spiritual teacher, Geshe Langritangpa made the spirit of enlightenment his quintessential practice and mainly taught the six Kadampa texts. He is the first Tibetan master to have written down these instructions for training the mind. The genre of texts called "stages of the path to enlightenment,"[29] *lamrim* in Tibetan, present the essence of the Buddha's teachings in an accessible form and make it quite clear how to practice. The so-called mind training texts, referred to as *lojong* in Tibetan, contain the core of those stages of the path. They focus on the development of the spirit of enlightenment and on the practice of giving and taking.

Geshe Chekawa,[30] the author of the *Seven Points for Training the Mind*, wrote one of the principal commentaries on Langritangpa's *Eight Verses* on which this teaching is based. He was born in eastern Tibet into a family of Nyingma[31] practitioners. He gained a good understanding and experience of both the old and new tantras,[32] was also skilled in dialectics and had read and understood the meaning of more than a hundred volumes of Buddhist scriptures. Despite this extensive knowledge he continued to feel that something was missing and that he had yet to discover the practice which would speed him towards enlightenment.

Eventually he came across the *Eight Verses* and felt so inspired and moved to faith by them that he decided to set out in search of their author to receive further instruction from him. When he arrived in central Tibet, Geshe Langritangpa had already passed away. However, he was told that Geshe Sharawa had intimate knowledge of how these eight verses were to be practiced.

At that time Geshe Sharawa was teaching Asanga's *Hearer Stages*. Geshe Chekawa listened to the teaching and was disappointed to hear nothing regarding the special instructions for transforming one's mind. He decided to find an opportunity to speak with Geshe Sharawa privately and to ask him whether he really possessed knowledge and experience regarding the *Eight Verses*. If he did not, Chekawa resolved to search for someone else who did.

One day Sharawa's students had been invited elsewhere for the midday meal and Chekawa found Sharawa alone, circumambulating a stupa set in a small copse of junipers. Diffidently he approached him, placed his long upper robe on the ground and invited the master to sit down. Sharawa declined to sit, saying that this was not a suitable place for teachings, and asked him what he wanted. Chekawa answered that he wanted to speak with him, to which Sharawa replied that he had said everything of importance while giving his public teachings. But on seeing that Chekawa was disconcerted by this answer, he agreed to sit down and, holding his string of beads made from the seeds of the *bodhi* tree[33] in his hand, he asked Chekawa what he really wanted.

Then Chekawa told him how he had come across the *Eight Verses* and how the words in the fifth verse, "May I accept defeat and offer the victory to them," had moved him deeply and been of great help to him. He wanted to know if this was something important and whether this teaching had a reliable source. Sharawa saw how earnest he was and told him decisively that whether or not these words had been helpful to him, the fact was that without putting them into practice, one could never attain enlightenment. As for the source of this teaching—who could doubt the authenticity of Nagarjuna? This teaching was based on Nagarjuna's words in the *Precious Garland*.[34]

Hearing this, Chekawa asked Sharawa to give him the complete instructions. Sharawa in turn asked him if he was prepared to stay and to practice intensively, to which Chekawa agreed. When he returned to the room where he was staying, he took out his copy of Nagarjuna's *Precious Garland* and there he found the words to which Sharawa had referred: "May their wrongdoing ripen on me and may my virtue ripen on them."

Chekawa remained with Sharawa for twelve years, during which he cultivated a relationship with him in the proper way, both in thought and in deed. He remained constantly aware of his spiritual master's kindness and served him in whatever ways he could. Relying on Sharawa's instructions he gained profound insights. Later he wrote:

> Disregarding suffering and ill repute,
> Because of my strong interest, I requested instruction
> On how to subdue misconceptions of the self.
> Now, if I die, I have no regrets.

He assumed that he must have been very familiar with these teachings for training the mind in a past life because, despite his scholarship, he had continued to feel that something important was lacking until Geshe Langritangpa's words had awakened in him deeply implanted imprints. He had at once felt a strong sense of conviction and never regretted the difficulties he had had to bear in order to receive the teaching on how to subdue selfishness. The kind of self-confidence which only comes from practice is apparent in his words, convincing proof that he had made the spirit of enlightenment his quintessential practice. Je Tsongkhapa too speaks of this in his *Abridged Stages of the Path*:[35]

> The spirit of enlightenment is
> The mainstay of the supreme vehicle,
> The foundation and basis of its powerful activities.
> Like an elixir that turns the two stores[36] to gold,
> It is a treasure of merit comprising every kind of good.
> Knowing this, heroic Bodhisattvas make this precious
> And supreme attitude their quintessential practice.

Greater kindheartedness can transform our daily life and make all our activities meaningful. This is something we can all practice whether or not we have extensive knowledge of philosophy.

Chapter Two

The Special Features of This Teaching

These special features are discussed in order to arouse interest in the teaching. As Geshe Chekawa points out at the beginning of his *Seven Points for Training the Mind*, the concise instructions for training the mind are like a diamond. Finding a diamond can completely rid us of poverty and allows us to fulfill all our wishes. Similarly, if we can take to heart all these instructions and develop both aspects of the spirit of enlightenment by putting them into practice, they will rid us completely of our spiritual poverty and allow us to fulfill our highest aims. Just as a fragment of a diamond outshines and is more precious than all other stones, practicing even one part of these instructions is extremely powerful and valuable. Simply arousing the spirit of enlightenment each time we do something positive will gradually have a transforming effect.

By developing the spirit of enlightenment we become Bodhisattvas and spiritual children of the enlightened ones. From the point of view of the family to which we now belong, we outshine even Hearer and Solitary Realizer Foe Destroyers[37] as well as those possessing the five types of super-knowledge,[38] who are capable of all sorts of miraculous feats. The spirit of enlightenment removes ordinary pain, sickness and poverty because the one who possesses it can use all difficulties to make it increase and grow.

Geshe Chekawa also compares these instructions to the sun. Darkness cannot hide or dull the brightness of the sun. Wherever the sun's light falls it drives out darkness, since darkness and sunlight cannot coexist in the same place. Similarly the whole of this teaching dispels the darkness of countless wrong ideas. Just as a single ray of sunlight can dispel darkness, practicing just one aspect of these instructions, by for instance developing greater compassion, will rid us of many misconceptions and selfish impulses, prevent disturbing emotions from arising and stop many negative actions.

When our love and compassion grow strong enough they will induce the spirit of enlightenment, and once this governs us, even our most ordinary actions will become positive. Bodhisattvas, who have gained control of their minds and in whom the spirit of enlightenment has become sufficiently powerful, can perform normally negative actions with only positive consequences. In his *Twenty Verses on the Bodhisattva Vow*[39] Chandragomin says:

> There is no fault if one has compassion,
> Because of love and a virtuous mind.

Of the ten harmful actions,[40] the three harmful mental activities—covetousness, harmful thoughts and wrong views—are always negative whenever they occur. For us ordinary people the three harmful physical actions of killing, stealing and sexual misconduct and the four negative verbal activities of lying, using harsh or abusive language, speaking divisively or indulging in meaningless talk are inevitably motivated by a negative state of mind. In the case of these great Bodhisattvas, since they engage in such actions only with the best intention of helping others, not only does this not involve any negativity but, on the contrary, it increases their store of merit and thereby contributes towards their enlightenment. Although we are not yet like them and must take great care about what we do, we have the potential to become Bodhisattvas ourselves, provided we train ourselves and gain mental control.

Shantideva compares the spirit of enlightenment to the sun and moon:

> It is the universal vehicle that saves
> All wandering beings from the states of loss—
> The rising moon of the enlightened mind
> That soothes the sorrows born of the afflictions.
> It is a mighty sun that utterly dispels
> The gloom and ignorance of wandering beings.[41]

Like the moon it cools the burning heat of the disturbing emotions and like the sun it illuminates the darkness caused by the obstructions to complete knowledge of all phenomena because it creates so much positive energy that one's understanding greatly increases. The disturbing emotions are like a terrible sickness that torments us and gives us no rest. When we develop the spirit of enlightenment we are no longer obsessed with ourselves, and all the emotions that grow out of our self-concern automatically grow weaker and weaker until they disappear.

The instructions for training the mind are also compared to a medicinal plant, every part of which—the roots, stem, leaves, flowers and fruit—are useful for healing different ailments. Similarly the two aspects of the spirit of enlightenment can cure us of our misconceptions, turbulent emotions and the compulsive actions induced by them which cause us suffering. Whereas there are many medicines for ordinary physical disorders, only spiritual practice can cure this mental sickness. The spirit of enlightenment is like a potent panacea.

If we could practice just one aspect of these instructions, for instance the patience of willingly accepting difficulties, it would transform our lives. Of course, if there is something we can do about the difficulties we encounter, our energy should be directed towards solving the problem. But there are times when others harm us, when our wishes are thwarted and we face trouble, disappointment or sickness and there is nothing we can do. Instead of getting upset we can view this as the outcome of our own past actions and understand that the negative momentum put in motion by those actions is ending through this unwanted experience. We can regard trouble as a broom that sweeps away much accumulated negativity.

Geshe Chekawa speaks of the instructions as being nectar-like. Normally poison is lethal and can kill us, but if we know how to handle toxic substances, they can become strengthening and even life-saving. The bad conditions which surround us at this time can rob us of all chances of attaining liberation, but if we know how to deal with them, they can help and support our inner development. Through these instructions we can turn poison into nectar!

We live in a troubled world where five kinds of "dregs"[42] are prevalent. Dregs are what is left when everything good and nourishing has been removed. Degenerate times is the first of the five dregs. This is a time of degeneration characterized by conflict and strife. Degenerate living beings are the second of the five. Those with few disturbing attitudes and emotions who are easy to help have already attained liberation, while those who still remain in cyclic existence are obstinate and difficult to deal with. We can see the truth of this when we consider ourselves and those around us.

Degenerate life span is the third. Although it appears that people are living longer than before, it is merely that some enjoy conducive conditions which allow them to remain alive for their complete life span. It is said that at one time human beings enjoyed much longer lives. Many people die an untimely death through disease or accidents and are unable to live out their full life span. They therefore do not have much opportunity to transform their minds through spiritual practice.

Degenerate disturbing emotions are the fourth of the dregs. At present our own and others' disturbing emotions and attitudes manifest in a very turbulent and intense way. The final degeneration is that of views. In Buddhism, "view" refers either to the correct view or understanding of reality, also called the supramundane correct view, or to the mundane or worldly correct view, the understanding of karma, the connection between actions and their effects. Neither the correct view of reality nor the correct view regarding the connection between actions and their effects is widely held at present. Instead many distorted and extremist ideas and ideologies prevail, and perverted forms of conduct are popular.

These different kinds of degeneration are increasing and becoming more widespread. Fewer and fewer people find happiness or create the causes which can give rise to it. Instead troubles and difficulties arising from external and internal causes abound. Few people think or do anything positive and most are governed by disturbing emotions. Not only is there more violence than ever between people, but human beings also inflict more harm on other forms of life. People's attitudes are perverse. They rejoice when others suffer and think it serves them right. Such thoughts prevent them from having any genuine altruism. When they see others prosper or do good in any way, they are tormented by envy, which prevents them from rejoicing at others' happiness.

It isn't surprising when ordinary people behave in this way, but when so-called practitioners are only preoccupied with this life and pursue reward, respect and recognition, it is clear that we have reached a sad state of affairs. Such attitudes cause competition and conflict between practitioners, who then disparage each other, which spoils their happiness and everyone else's, makes it impossible to do what is virtuous and is a cause of despair for those who observe their behavior.

What hope is left when those who claim to be practitioners behave in this way? And what is sadder than conflict between adherents of different faiths? Spiritual practice is the root of all happiness and well-being in the world and such conflict destroys that root. The founders of the great religions were surely intent on helping us to overcome our troubles and find peace and were not motivated by partisan agendas.

The physical environment is full of the results of our negative actions. Harvests fail or decline, medicines lose their power to cure, natural resources are running out, food lacks nutritiousness, there is an upsurge of new diseases and old ones take a more virulent form. Thieves and criminals are on the increase and people are more deceitful and exploitative than ever before. The physical elements are out of balance and natural disasters abound. There is a plethora of negative internal and external conditions.

At such a time practice of these instructions is of great importance because it allows us to transform all these adverse factors into circumstances conducive to the attainment of enlightenment. If we learn how to do this, the more difficult our situation becomes, the more useful it will prove to our spiritual growth. Just as a fire burns hotter the more fuel there is, so difficult conditions simply make a true practitioner of mind training stronger. If we can transform these difficulties and make them into our path, we will be able to remain serene and happy no matter what happens. Even if we can't turn everything into a cause for complete enlightenment, it would make such a difference if we could be a little more calm and positive in our response to difficulties.

The purpose of these instructions for practice is twofold. The ultimate purpose is to insure that all living beings find lasting happiness by attaining non-abiding nirvana,[43] the most complete and highest form of enlightenment. The temporary purpose is to equip us with everything needed to fulfill this aim. In order to help all living beings reach enlightenment, we must attain enlightenment ourselves. This means we have to practice the extensive deeds of Bodhisattvas, in particular the six perfections, without which enlightenment is impossible. We will only do this if we cherish others more than ourselves. Our practice of the six perfections will not lead to enlightenment unless we are motivated by the highest form of altruism. Without sufficient interest in the two aspects of the spirit of enlightenment, we will not make the effort to practice, but if our spirit of enlightenment is strong enough, everything else will follow naturally.

This strength will not develop unless we first awaken our Mahayana disposition[44] through training ourselves to cherish others and through repeatedly arousing love and compassion. Only an intense interest in the profound and extensive paths of Mahayana practice and a heartfelt wish to be of use to others will cause our Mahayana disposition to awaken. This must occur before we can set out on the Mahayana paths of practice.

It would be impossible to awaken the Mahayana disposition if it did not exist within us. All living beings have this precious potential, which is twofold. From the point of view of the Chittamatra[45] school of philosophy, the innately abiding disposition[46] is the potential of mental consciousness to be freed from all stains and to develop inconceivable positive qualities. It is the potential for developing an uncontaminated mental state,[47] which awakens when the right cooperative conditions, such as hearing, thinking and meditating on the teachings, occur. For this school of thought the developmental disposition[48] refers to the activated potential when positive development takes place. Thus, from the Chittamatra point of view, both aspects of this disposition are impermanent phenomena, produced by causes and conditions.

Here, however, we will follow the Madhyamika[49] view, according to which the innately abiding disposition, possessed by all living beings, is the clear light nature[50] of the mind, namely its emptiness of inherent existence, which is its fundamental nature. The developmental disposition refers to the clear and cognizant nature of the mind, the seed for development and for the growth of positive qualities such as faith and conviction, a real wish for freedom from cyclic existence, love and compassion. There is no difference between the fundamental nature of our mind and the fundamental nature of an enlightened being's mind, but at present our mind is clouded by certain pollutant factors. Nevertheless, these are temporary and can be removed.

To help us understand this our mind is compared to water, to the sky and to gold. The pollutants in water are not an integral part of it but are extraneous in that they come from other sources. Because water is pure by nature, the pollutants can be removed. When clouds appear in the sky, they are not part of it. When they disappear, the sky is clear again. Gold may be alloyed with other metals, but after it is refined the gold once more becomes pure because that is its nature.

The clear and cognizant nature of our mind is pure from the beginning and has always been free of true existence. At present our mind is affected by ignorance because of which everything appears to us as truly or inherently existent. This ignorance distorts our view. All our misconceptions and their imprints and all obstructions can be removed by developing the ultimate spirit of enlightenment.

This should give us great hope. Sometimes our habits make us despair of ever changing and we feel stuck, but with sufficient effort and application of the right antidotes, we can definitely bring about positive changes. The presence of this disposition within us is not something Buddhists have invented but is a fact. Imagine that there is a precious treasure buried under the ground and we are living right on top of it. We have no idea it's there. Then someone with a divining rod or clairvoyant powers alerts us to the presence of the treasure. Of course, we would start digging right away and would feel overjoyed when we finally unearthed it.

Gold mines, diamond mines, copper mines and other resources run out sooner or later, but this treasure-like disposition can never be exhausted. It is the source of all happiness and the more we use it, the more there is. We are not aware of how much happiness it can bring us and others. The mind's fundamental nature is emptiness and every moment of mental activity depends on a multitude of factors. It is because of this that we can free ourselves from faults and develop undreamed-of qualities and abilities.

Chapter Three

Awakening Our Mahayana Disposition

As with all other practices, doing what will awaken our Mahayana disposition involves preparation, the actual activity and the appropriate conclusion. To prepare ourselves we must think extensively about the preciousness of our human life, about impermanence and about the connection between actions and their effects.

Make ready a comfortable meditation seat. When the Buddha Shakyamuni attained complete enlightenment, the ground beneath him became diamond hard and indestructible. This is represented by the swastika[51] that you draw with grains of rice or with chalk under your meditation cushion. It denotes the wish to attain stability in your practice. On the swastika lay some *kusha* grass.[52] If you have several of these long stems, place them in a circle with the tips towards the center. If you have only one stem, lay it on the swastika pointing forwards in the direction you intend to face when seated. The long soft fronds of the *kusha* grass remain untangled, symbolizing a clear and unconfused state of mind. When the Buddha Shakyamuni was preparing to sit in meditation under the *bodhi* tree, he asked a seller of *kusha* grass to give him some and he used it make the seat on which he later attained enlightenment. Laying this grass under your cushion denotes your wish to emulate the Buddha. Also under your cushion lay some couch grass[53] which you have formed into a circle. Couch grass has many segments, symbolizing a long life. The presence of these different kinds of grass also indicates contentment with a simple life. The cushion which you place on the swastika and grasses should be slightly raised at the back. This will help you to keep your spine straight.

Now sit on this comfortable seat in a good meditation posture. The position of Vairochana,[54] which has seven features, is considered ideal for meditation. Sit with your legs in the *vajra* position.[55] This creates an auspicious precedent for attaining the *vajra* position of the energy channels, energies and constituents during the stage of completion in the practice of tantra. Although this position is initially not easy to hold, it can be maintained for long periods once one is accustomed to it. Keeping the lower part of the body locked in this way prevents ailments caused by cold. The upper part of the body should be as relaxed as possible to prevent disturbances caused by the different types of energies.

Place your hands in the position of meditative equipoise four finger-widths below the navel, with the back of the right hand resting on the palm of the left. Your thumbs touch, thereby creating a triangle. This position of the hands symbolizes activation of the inner fire centered at the navel.[56] Keep your elbows away from the body to allow a flow of air under your arms. This prevents slackness and lethargy in meditation.

Keep your spine straight to bring the energy channels into the best position for free movement of the energies. Slightly tuck in your chin to inhibit the upward-flowing energies, which can cause agitation when uncontrolled. Your mouth should be neither open nor tightly closed but relaxed, with the tip of your tongue touching the upper palate behind your front teeth. This prevents thirst and drooling during long periods of meditative absorption.

Do not open your eyes wide, as it encourages distraction. On the other hand do not close them completely because, though you may feel more concentrated at the beginning, this can easily lead to sleepiness. Focus them loosely in line with the tip of your nose.

Now relax your body and mind and arouse a special motivation—the spirit of enlightenment. Think that all living beings have been your mothers throughout the limitless rebirths you have taken. They have nurtured and shown you kindness just as your mother of this life has done. At present they are suffering and are constantly creating the causes for more suffering, which means they have no opportunity to experience happiness. It is your responsibility to help them because you have been their child over and over again and owe them so much. They need your help but at the moment you are incapable of helping them effectively. Only an enlightened person can, since every action and every breath of an enlightened being, every ray of light that such a person emanates, helps living beings. From this it is clear that if you really want to help them in the most effective ways, you must attain enlightenment.

Imagine before you a lion throne, neither to the right nor to the left, not too high nor too low but level with the center of your brow. It should be far enough away to allow you to make a full prostration before it. If it is too high and you feel that you need to look up, it will disturb the upward-flowing energies and can lead to excitement and distraction. Imagining it too low can encourage slackness and lethargy and is disrespectful to the field of accumulation[57] that you imagine upon the throne.

The throne is supported at each corner by a lion. These lions symbolize the ten powers[58] and four states of fearlessness[59] of an enlightened being. One can also imagine eight lions, two at each corner, representing the eight sovereign qualities.[60] The lions have all four feet on the ground and support the throne on the nape of their necks. Their heads are turned to the right and left as though they are keeping watch. Their tails are hidden under the throne. Think of them not as statues but as living, breathing lions with bright tawny eyes, sharp fangs and claws and shining lustrous manes. Their torsos are strong and their hindquarters tight and muscular. They are fully grown, powerful and frightening to behold. It is said that when the Buddha attained enlightenment, Bodhisattvas on the ten stages manifested as lions and supported his throne. Just as lions intimidate other animals, so the Buddha and his retinue intimidate worldly gods and those who are hostile to the teachings.

To concentrate your attention you may imagine the throne to be quite small yet it easily accommodates the whole field of accumulation. On the other hand, it can also be imagined as vast and expansive. When you look at it, it seems to be in front but actually it extends everywhere. It is made of silver, gold or lapis and studded with valuable jewels. This signifies the great value and rarity of the field of accumulation in our world.

On this throne rests a lotus. Just as the lotus is untainted by the mud from which it grows, those on the throne are untouched by the faults of cyclic existence. The lotus represents the paths of insight of the initial and intermediate levels of practice, which form the preparation and basis for the Mahayana practices associated with the mind training tradition.

Lying on top of the lotus is a moon. When both sun and moon are present, they represent the two aspects of the spirit of enlightenment—the conventional and ultimate. The presence of the lotus, sun and moon together indicate that those seated upon them have perfected the wish for freedom, the spirit of enlightenment and the correct view of reality. Imagining this is auspicious for our own acquisition of these insights.

With the wish to gain enlightenment for the sake of all living beings, imagine before you the field of accumulation, visualizing your spiritual teacher in the form of Avalo-kiteshvara[61] or, following the Kadampa masters, as the Buddha Amitabha in the form of an emanation body (see Appendix II).

Amitabha is visualized with one head and two arms, seated in the *vajra* position. His hands support a begging bowl full of the nectar of immortality.[62] The back of his right hand rests on the palm of his left hand in the gesture of meditative equipoise. He is red and radiant, the color of a ruby mountain illuminated by a hundred thousand suns. Red denotes powerful activity, in this case control over life span.

He is surrounded by Bodhisattvas, among them Avalo-kiteshvara and Vajrapani.[63] He and the Bodhisattvas around him have a white *OM* at their foreheads, a red *AH* at their throats and a blue *HUNG* at their hearts.[64] The *HUNG* at their hearts emanates rays of light which invite wisdom beings[65] from all directions. These enter Amitabha and the Bodhi-sattvas, who become the embodiment of all objects of refuge.

Perform the seven-part practice,[66] beginning with obei-sance. Make beautiful real and imagined offerings, confess all that you have done wrong throughout time and apply the four counteractions.[67] Rejoice in the good deeds and happiness of others without resentment or envy and also rejoice in your own virtue and in the good you have done. Request your teachers to remove the darkness of ignorance by lighting the lamp of the teachings and request them to remain in the world. Finally dedicate your virtue to act as a cause for the enlightenment of all living beings.

Then offer the *mandala*[68] and make requests: request that your mind should turn fully towards the teachings, that your practice should become a true path,[69] that you will meet with no obstacles on that path and that you will be able to develop love and compassion.

Once when Geshe Langritangpa was meditating, a mouse tried to remove a large turquoise from his mandala but the turquoise was too big to fit into its mouth. He watched it run back into the hole from which it had come. After a few moments it returned with four other mice. One mouse lay down on its back and the others managed to heave the turquoise onto its stomach. The four then pushed and pulled the recumbent mouse till they had transported the turquoise to their hole. Geshe Langritangpa, who normally was quite serious, is said to have laughed loud and long at their resourcefulness.

At present we have very little inclination to practice and whatever virtue we have created in the past has been directed towards finding happiness in this life and protecting ourselves from suffering. We have done nothing meaningful that can help us in future lives. When we ask for blessings so that our mind may turn fully towards the teachings, we do so with the wish that whatever virtue we create will be oriented not to the well-being of this life but to that of future lives.

Our practice becomes a true path when it does not act as a cause for further rebirth in cyclic existence, no matter how excellent, but becomes a cause for complete liberation. We ask for blessings that our practice may be accompanied by a genuine wish for liberation because we have recognized that cyclic existence is like a fiery furnace.

Our principal obstacle is self-concern, which could make us seek liberation for ourselves alone and would thus prevent us from attaining complete enlightenment free from the fears associated with worldly existence and with a state of personal peace. We ask for blessings that our practice, which is directed towards freedom, may bring true benefit to us and others and lead to unsurpassable enlightenment.

We also ask for help in getting rid of all negative states of mind, beginning with wrong attitudes and disrespect towards our spiritual teachers through to our misconceptions regarding the actual nature of the self and other phenomena. We request that we may quickly develop insights and positive states of mind, from cherishing our spiritual teachers in the correct way through to the union of no more learning,[70] namely the state of highest enlightenment.

If we cannot overcome our preoccupation with the well-being of this life, we will never succeed in finding freedom, since our hopes for success and happiness and fears of failure and unhappiness prevent a true wish for freedom from arising. Our concern with approval, rewards, respect and our reputation tethers us to cyclic existence like a calf tethered to a wooden post.

Once when Geshe Potowa was staying in Reting he watched a young calf that was tethered to a post by a long rope. The calf heard its mother's distant call and immediately set off at a run, entirely forgetting about the rope. You could see that it felt it would soon reach its mother, but when it had gone some way, the rope jerked it back so hard that it fell over and after that it ran round and round, until the whole rope was tightly wound around the post, which was now right under the calf's chin, so that it couldn't move.

Watching this Geshe Potowa thought how similar it was to the way we practice. We set out full of good intentions, perhaps becoming ordained, and after some years, when we are doing quite well and think we have accomplished something, we are jerked back by the rope of worldly concerns. Our preoccupation with the well-being of this life, with our body and possessions, with our relations or followers grows stronger than ever before. We become arrogant and forget about the teachings and are worse than we were before we began. In fact we haven't got anywhere at all with our practice.

If the post is pulled out or the rope is cut, the calf is set free and can run straight to its mother. Similarly, if we can sever our attachment to the well-being of this life by thinking about impermanence and the imminence of death, we will be able to practice purely.

Obstacles to our practice may be external, internal or secret. The external ones consist of natural disasters, harm inflicted by human and nonhuman beings, sicknesses and so forth. Internal obstacles are our own disturbed states of mind and emotions and all the obstructions to liberation and full knowledge of all phenomena. Secret obstacles are seemingly good circumstances, which distract the practitioner and make him or her forget about practice. For instance, one might gain

a good reputation as a sincere practitioner and thereby attract followers and wealth, which in the end make one neglect one's practice.

When you have requested blessings so that your mind
may really turn towards the teachings, that your practice
may become a true path and that you may be free from obstacles, your spiritual teacher in the form of Amitabha and
his retinue of Bodhisattvas are greatly pleased. The retinue
dissolves into light which enters Amitabha. Seated on his
throne he comes to the top of your head and you once more
perform the seven-part practice. Then imagine him remaining there and begin your meditation.

Chapter Four

The Supremacy of Others

In order to become enlightened we must engage in the ineffable activities of Bodhisattvas, but no matter how long we attempt to do this, we will never succeed unless we can exchange self and others, that is, reverse our present attitudes. This is the root of all the skillful means we hope to develop and is the main training undertaken by true practitioners of the Great Vehicle. The ability to bring about such a switch in attitudes depends upon constantly seeing all living beings as supreme.

1   **May I always cherish all beings**
       With the resolve to accomplish for them
       The highest good that is more precious
       Than any wish-fulfilling jewel.

"I" here refers to each of us and does not just refer to the author. The implication is that we should regard the teachings as personally relevant. "All beings" refers to those we view as our friends, those we view as enemies and those towards whom we have neither feelings of attachment nor hostility. If we could feel love, compassion and the spirit of enlightenment in relation to every living being, without excluding even one, that spirit of enlightenment would be more precious than any wish-fulfilling jewel. When we pray to a wish-fulfilling jewel, it grants our wishes. In the same way, the spirit of enlightenment fulfills both our own and others' temporary wishes and will grant us lasting happiness in the form of complete enlightenment. Our motivation should be based on the certainty that this is so.

Think, "May I always cherish living beings as supreme and may I constantly be concerned for their well-being." When we truly love all living beings without distinguishing between them and feel so compassionate towards them that the spirit of enlightenment arises spontaneously, all our short-term and long-term wishes and aims will be fulfilled. As you think in this way, your spiritual teacher in the form of Amitabha expresses his joy by sending down a flow of nectar and light which enters you and washes away everything negative. As the nectar and light continue to flow, your life-force, positive energy and good qualities increase.

We are in the habit of neglecting and ignoring other living beings. By recognizing their preciousness, by valuing and cherishing them, we will experience both immediate and ultimate happiness. If on the other hand we continue to cherish only ourselves and neglect, disparage and demean others, the result will be everything that we do not want. As Shantideva says in his *Way of the Bodhisattva*:

> The worlds of beings are a Buddhafield,
> Thus the Mighty Lord has taught.
> For many who have sought the happiness of others
> Have gone beyond, attaining to perfection.[71]

Living beings, our mothers, are the source of everything good and excellent in the world. Cherishing them all equally is the root of Mahayana practice. How can we develop love, compassion and the spirit of enlightenment without living beings? They are like a fertile field. If we sow good seed in a fertile field and then tend it well, we will reap an abundant harvest. Once we realize the value of our field, we will look after it carefully because we know that it can give us a good crop. Living beings are our field. If we do what will develop our love and compassion for them and practice the six perfections and the four ways of helping others to become mature[72] with the spirit of enlightenment, the harvest we will gather is our own and others' highest good. When we recognize living beings as the source of everything we wish for, we will appreciate them, be concerned about them and feel personally affected when they suffer in any way. We will see them as lovable and appealing and show them respect and affection.

In so far as we find everything we desire now in our present life through other living beings, they are like wish-fulfilling jewels. If we affix a wish-fulfilling jewel to the top of a victory banner and if we pray and make requests and offerings to it, it can grant us a long life, good health and riches. Similarly, as a result of regarding others as more precious than ourselves, by showing them respect and being generous to them, we will enjoy a long life, freedom from sickness and increasing wealth.

When we consider the future, living beings are far more precious to us than any wish-granting jewel could possibly be. Even a hundred thousand such jewels cannot affect our future lives, for when we die, we must leave them and everything we own behind. But cherishing and protecting living beings and developing generosity and patience towards them will insure that we have a strong body and mind, good dwelling places and surroundings as well as possessions and wealth. In the meantime these will all be of benefit to us. Ultimately through such conduct we will develop the love and compassion which lead to the spirit of enlightenment and to complete illumination itself.

In the *Sutra Which Thoroughly Reveals the Teachings*[73] the Buddha said that the field of living beings is the field of Buddhas. This implies that both are equally important to us and that we should venerate ordinary living beings as much as we do enlightened ones. Shantideva's *Way of the Bodhisattva* also makes this clear:

> Thus the state of Buddhahood depends
> On beings and the Buddhas equally.
> By what tradition is it then
> That Buddhas, but not beings, are revered?[74]

It often seems that our disturbing emotions and self-concern are simply too strong and that we will never be able to put others' interests before our own. However, we should not be discouraged because everything becomes easier with practice, and as Shantideva says:

> There's nothing that does not grow light
> Through habit and familiarity.[75]

Appreciating the true value of other living beings, cherishing them and seeing them as lovable will make us less angry and more patient. We must constantly remind ourselves that they are just like us: they crave happiness and want to avoid suffering at all costs. They long to be cherished as much as we do.

It is entirely in our hands whether we make use of our freedom from constraints and the many conducive conditions we enjoy to gain the lasting happiness of enlightenment or to do what will bring us suffering in bad rebirths. We can determine our future, which depends on our state of mind. The Buddha said: "I am my own protector. No other can protect me. The wise who make excellent effort will attain high status."

Nagarjuna reminds us that liberation means freedom from bondage, and that such freedom is the result of our own efforts. In his *Letter to a Friend*[76] he says:

> Liberation depends on us, and for that
> Nobody can give us help.
> So with learning, ethics and concentration:
> Make effort to understand the four truths.

If we work with our mind and direct it towards virtue, we will gain the highest well-being and happiness. If we leave our mind as it is and make no effort to discipline it, we will gravitate towards nonvirtue and this will lead to suffering in bad rebirths.

In order to accomplish our own and others' highest good, we must train ourselves by not allowing our disturbing emotions to dominate us and by constantly redirecting our attention towards that which is positive. Positive here refers to love, compassion and the spirit of enlightenment. Developing these positive states of mind for our own sake—to make us feel better or so that we can in some way benefit from them—cannot lead to an excellent and unsurpassable result because we are still motivated by self-interest. Altruism and concern for others must come from the very depths of our hearts.

One of the main obstacles is our pride. This pride is an inflated state of mind and relies on our false view of the transitory collection, which focuses on the existent self, attributed to our body and mind, and distorts it. When we are on top of a very high mountain, we look down on all the lower peaks. Similarly, when we are full of pride, everyone else appears lower. We are the best and everyone else is inferior. This pride is associated with our self-preoccupation and makes us act inappropriately and disrespectfully towards others, thereby bringing us face to face with all kinds of unpleasant and unwanted experiences. As long as we feel and act as though we are the center of the universe, we will never develop real concern for others. To counteract this attitude we train ourselves always to think of them as supremely important by considering their good qualities and by reviewing our own faults and weaknesses.

We may protest that we do not think of ourselves as exceptional nor feel that we possess particularly good qualities and for that reason lack pride, but pride can be hard to recognize. In his *Treasury of Knowledge* Vasubandhu identifies different kinds of pride.[77] There is pride that makes one feel superior towards inferiors and pride towards equals where one thinks oneself better than they are. One can also feel pride towards someone superior, since pride distorts reality and does not accord with fact. There is pride in relation to one's body and mind which makes one feel an exaggerated sense of identity. There is the pride of thinking one is great when in fact one doesn't possess any noteworthy qualities or insights. There is pride in relation to those who are vastly superior to oneself, through which one feels only marginally inferior to them, and there is pride in faults which one mistakes for good qualities. When we understand all these different kinds of pride and then examine ourselves, we may be surprised to discover that we are, in fact, a ball of pride. Dromtönpa said that the water of good qualities runs off a ball of pride.

Others will find us hard to get along with while we remain reluctant to acknowledge their good qualities and show them respect. The instructions of our spiritual teachers can make little impact as long as we are self-centered. Geshe Chengawa rebuked his students for their pride, saying, "Look to see where the green shows up first in spring—on the high mountains or in the valleys?" All rivers automatically flow down to the land at sea level because it is lower. Unless we have enough humility to take the lowest seat, we will never develop worldly or supramundane insights. So to overcome our pride we must learn to cherish others and put ourselves last.

2.   **Whenever I am in the company of others,**
      May I regard myself as inferior to all
      And from the depths of my heart
      Cherish others as supreme.

Whoever we are with—inferiors, equals or superiors—and wherever we are, allowing others to be of supreme importance, regarding our own status, wealth and good qualities as less important than theirs and sincerely respecting them is the way to get rid of pride. This opens the door to happiness and to the true development of our own potential.

None of us feels happy when we are full of pride. We become hypersensitive and easily feel threatened. We are envious of others who are in any way superior, compete with our equals and are supercilious and condescending towards inferiors. Our conduct expresses these attitudes and creates personal conflicts and problems in society at large. Our pride seems justified but though we may indeed possess good qualities, that is not a valid reason for pride. We only need to consider those who are wealthier, more distinguished, more educated, more beautiful, more healthy or vigorous. This will help us to see things in better perspective.

Conceit can arise on account of our knowledge, power, strength, conduct, generosity, ethical life-style, attractiveness, happiness or even just our fine singing voice or the way we cook! Our self-preoccupation prevents us from making any real progress. Nagarjuna in his *Letter to a Friend* suggests a way to overcome this:

> We are not free from sickness, ageing and death,
> Nor from losing what we love, and also not from
> Responsibility for our actions—thinking of this repeatedly
> Prevents conceit through its antidote.

Our happiness and suffering depend on our previous actions and we have no control over these. Involuntarily we experience pain and suffering because they are the result of our own past negative actions. Nor can we control how much happiness we experience, since it, too, is the consequence of our actions.

Therefore in meditation we should remind ourselves again and again to take the back seat and to contemplate our own faults and others' good qualities. This does not mean we should allow others to exploit and manipulate us. When this occurs or there is any danger that it could occur, it is important to prevent it in as peaceful a way as possible.

The first verse instructs us always to see others as lovable and appealing. This counteracts our anger and hostility and is related to the practice of patience. The second verse instructs us to consider our own faults and to practice humility. This counters attachment to ourselves, which makes us do many harmful things in the pursuit of happiness, and therefore is related to the practice of ethical discipline. As long as we cherish ourselves most, we will not be able to put others in this position of supremacy.

Shantideva says:

> Wanting what is best for me—
> Stupidity and lower realms result!
> Let this be changed, applied to others—
> Honors and the realms of bliss will come![78]

Our craving for more rewards, praise and respect and for a better reputation than others enjoy will only lead to a bad rebirth, an unattractive appearance, inferior status and stupidity. If we insure that others enjoy these very things, we too will enjoy them and much more in the future.

Since these instructions for training the mind belong to the teachings of the Great Vehicle, it is vital to approach them without pride. We can make a travesty of this practice through pride in being a practitioner of mind-training. To insure that this doesn't happen we must keep constant watch on our mind. Everything a true practitioner does becomes an opportunity for mental training.

Thus in all our actions we should consider ourselves inferior to others, and whether they are good, bad or mediocre, we should give them paramount importance. The texts tell us we should feel like the child of a servant at the king's court. That child has no delusions of grandeur. Or we should be like the carpet on the floor—in the lowest possible position. These are attitudes that must come from the depths of our heart as we contemplate the good qualities of others, hold them supreme, show them respect and prevent ourselves from acting improperly towards them. It is said that a

Bodhisattva should constantly look at others with the wish
to help them, with the wish for their happiness, with feelings of affection and with the attitude that they are his or
her teachers. In order to do all this we must be mindful and
mentally alert all the time—whether we are walking, stand-
ing, sitting or lying down.

Chapter Five

Dealing with the Foe

We must learn to notice at once any thought or feeling associated with the three poisonous emotions of desire, anger and confusion and remind ourselves instantly that these emotions are our bitter enemies and will only hurt us and others.

3.   In all my actions may I watch my mind,
        And as soon as disturbing emotions arise,
        May I forcefully stop them at once,
        Since they will hurt both me and others.

In a gentle but energetic way, remembering that these thoughts and feelings are not inherently existent, we should stop them immediately.

As has already been mentioned, concern for others and seeing them as lovable is helpful in preventing anger, while considering oneself inferior helps to prevent feelings of attachment to oneself. In this verse Geshe Langritangpa tells us what to do when these emotions do arise. He advises us to stop them at once before they gather momentum.

What kind of harm do they do? We must investigate what effect they have on us. They make our mind disturbed, turbulent and unclear as a result of which we engage with and respond to things in a faulty and distorted way. Each time they occur, the predisposition for these disturbing emotions becomes more firmly entrenched, which insures their continuity.

In his *Great Treatise on the Stages of the Path* Je Tsongkhapa defines ten disturbing emotions and attitudes as follows.[79] He describes how attachment or desire, which focuses on external and internal[80] attractive and pleasurable objects, is as hard to get rid of as oil which has soaked into a piece of cloth. The stain made by even a small drop of oil quickly grows and spreads. Once attachment or desire is active, it tends to grow and we soon have difficulty in separating from the object of our attachment.

Hostility or anger is directed towards living beings, pain, weapons or different aspects of the environment, which are seen as sources of suffering. It is a rough and malevolent state of mind characterized by the wish to harm.

There isn't a single one of us who has never felt hostile and angry, so we know about the effects of anger. Does it make us feel better or worse? It stirs us up, makes us miserable and destroys our tranquillity. It is quite easy to recognize anger as a foe and to see how it harms us because its destructiveness is apparent. But we find it much harder and are also reluctant to acknowledge the harm done by attachment because it is a foe masquerading as a friend. When desire or attachment first arises, it feels quite pleasurable but eventually it lands us in trouble. It wants to possess what it has fabricated and we reach out for something which, in fact, does not exist. Failure to get what we want frustrates us and anger quickly follows. The third of the poisons, confusion or ignorance, simply stimulates desire and anger and lies at the root of all the disturbing emotions.

When we are very angry, we feel unhappy and then, as we lash out physically or verbally, others become unhappy too. Not only that but through our anger we create causes for future suffering. Anger, envy and pride prevent us from developing genuine concern for others. Anger spoils our happiness and as a result of it we may even lose money and property. Anger makes us feel paranoid when we are with others and may result in all kinds of delusions regarding their behavior towards us.

Pride depends upon our misconception of the "I" and "mine," referred to as the false view of the transitory collection. This inflated feeling of superiority may focus on what is internal or external, high or low, good or bad.

Ignorance is an unclear state of mind which misunderstands how things exist, such as the Three Jewels, the four noble truths and the connection between actions and their effects. Like ignorance, doubt may focus on the same topics and is a state of ambivalence as to whether they really are as described or not.

The false view of the transitory collection is a deluded understanding which focuses on the validly existent "I" and "mine" attributed to the five aggregates and sees them as a truly existent "I" and "mine." Extreme views also focus on the validly existent self and consider it either eternal and unchanging or as discontinuing and subject to annihilation. These are also deluded forms of understanding.

Belief in the supremacy of mistaken views focuses on and considers the false view of the transitory collection, an extreme view or a wrong view as supreme.

Belief in the supremacy of codes of discipline and conduct is a deluded understanding that holds inferior forms of discipline, physical and verbal behavior, dress, conventions and the physical and mental aggregates of one who follows such discipline and conduct as supreme. It is based on the belief that these forms of behavior are a means of purifying wrongdoing, overcoming the disturbing emotions and gaining freedom from cyclic existence.

Wrong views are a deluded form of understanding that denies the existence of such things as past and future lives and the connection between actions and their effects or asserts, for instance, that the cause of living beings is a divine creator or primal matter.

These and the other disturbing attitudes and emotions stop us from finding happiness, and if we allow them to rule us we will soon gain a bad reputation. There is no doubt that this attracts the disapprobation of all who protect and practice the teachings, but far from turning their back on us, they recognize from our self-destructive behavior that we need extra care.

If we indulge these disturbing emotions and allow ourselves to be ruled by any of these attitudes, they will do nothing but harm us and others, now and in the future. They are our real enemies, enslaving us and robbing us of our freedom. We are governed by our minds and at present our minds are governed by disturbing emotions. Shantideva says:

> Anger, lust—these enemies of mine—
> Are limbless and devoid of faculties.
> They have no bravery, no cleverness;
> How then have they reduced me to such slavery?[81]

Though they are neither strong nor astute, we nevertheless allow them to dominate us. How can anyone be happy when in the power of an enemy?

A conventional enemy may harm us, but patience and a refusal to retaliate can bring us benefit both in this life and in the future. However, tolerance towards these hostile disturbing emotions and attempts at peaceful coexistence with them will never bring us any reward. They will do us nothing but harm if we don't take steps to drive them out. No conventional enemy can do us such harm. The most an ordinary enemy can do is to defeat us for a short space of time or destroy us in this life, but the disturbing emotions will insure our misery for many lifetimes to come. Shantideva says:

> All other foes that I appease and wait upon
> Will show me favors, give me every aid,
> But should I serve my dark defiled emotions,
> They will only harm me, draw me down to grief.[82]

We can hold talks, make concessions, reach an agreement and sign a treaty with a conventional enemy, but it is utterly useless to befriend and make concessions to the disturbing emotions. It is important to foster good relations with others and to sustain our relationships with them for as long as possible, but we should break off all relations with the disturbing emotions as quickly as possible. They injure us both physically and mentally, spoil our happiness and bring nothing but pain. Once we have taken rebirth in any of the unfortunate states, there will be no opportunity to get rid of them.

Geshe Potowa reminds us that we have been reborn in cyclic existence again and again as a result of these disturbing emotions and the actions they cause. So far they have never left us alone, nor will they ever leave of their own accord. The only way to get rid of them is to make an effort now while we have this precious human life of freedom and fortune.[83]

The first Dalai Lama, the great Gyelwa Gendun Drup,[84] said:

> Think generally of the kindness of beings and specially
> Foster pure perception of all practitioners.
> Subdue disturbing emotions, the foe dwelling within.

We all want happiness and no suffering. Since the disturbing emotions are the root of our suffering, we must rid ourselves of them. On the other hand, kindheartedness and understanding are the root of happiness, which is why it is worth making every effort to develop and enhance these qualities. Even though they have afflicted us throughout all our lives, we can get rid of the disturbing emotions because they are based on distorted perception and false reasons. The feelings and insights that are capable of dislodging them are, on the contrary, based on very sound reasons.

For success in taming our mind we must be vigilant and capable of identifying the disturbing emotions, recognizing how they function and what will act as an effective antidote.

This is the heart of the Buddha's teaching. We don't practice for the Buddha or for our spiritual teachers but for ourselves. However, if we practice sincerely in this way, enlightened beings will be pleased because by doing this we sow the seeds of happiness and get rid of the roots of suffering, which is what they want for us.

The pleasure and pain that this body experiences are the results of past actions. The pleasure and pain we will experience in the future depend on our present state of mind. Unwanted future suffering is the result of negative thoughts and actions; therefore, be merciless in uprooting them. The pleasure and happiness we desire are caused by positive thoughts and actions, so take great care to foster them.

Since our state of mind is the decisive factor, we must constantly safeguard our mind, directing it towards what is constructive and away from what is negative. This is done by employing mindfulness to keep our attention on what is positive and watchfulness to spot any negative impulses, whether physical, verbal or mental, the moment they begin. Without these two mental activities it is impossible to protect our mind. Shantideva says:

> All you who would protect your minds,
> Maintain awareness and your mental vigilance.
> Guard them both, at cost of life and limb—
> Thus I join my hands, beseeching you.[85]

The only way to drive out the disturbing emotions is by recognizing them and applying effective antidotes. The ordinary antidotes involve states of mind which are diametrically opposed to the disturbing emotions. For instance, strong desire, which regards the object towards which it is directed as extremely attractive, can be countered by contemplating the flaws and unappealing aspects of the object. Likewise, strong anger, which wishes to destroy its object, is countered by love, compassion and the wish to help. Anger is incompatible with these feelings and cannot coexist with them.

In the context of the *Eight Verses for Training the Mind*, pride, which is one of the main obstacles to cherishing others, is countered by assuming the lowest position. Other texts tell us that pride, particularly in one's knowledge, should be dealt with by thinking about the process of dependent arising, about the twelve sources and eighteen constituents.[86] There is so much we don't know—even the inside of our own body is a mystery to us.

There are in this way specific antidotes to counteract specific disturbing emotions, all of which are included in the practices associated with the three levels of capacity. The antidote to all the disturbing emotions is the understanding of how things exist at their most fundamental level. This counteracts the misconceptions from which the disturbing emotions arise.

Our task is thus quite clear but we find it extremely difficult to undertake because we are so accustomed to living with these emotions. They arise before we realize what is happening and once they gather momentum they are virtually impossible to control, since the antidotes at our disposal are still very weak. For this reason it is considered wise for us beginners to avoid contact with things that act as catalysts for these emotions. When the conditions are incomplete, the emotions will not arise. And so it is often recommended that we seek seclusion—physical seclusion from a busy life and mental seclusion from busy thoughts.

If we are at home when one of the disturbing emotions arises, we can deal with it in a variety of ways: we can make a mandala offering to our spiritual teacher and request blessings in order to have enough strength to resist and calm this emotion. We can also meditate, focusing our entire attention on our breath as we inhale and exhale. We may also try thinking of something else to distract ourselves or go for a walk until the emotion dies down. Then, during our meditation, we can think about the antidote and try to apply it. In seclusion we cultivate the ultimate counteraction, which is the understanding of selflessness. However, Bodhisattvas do not necessarily seek the physical seclusion of an isolated place but cultivate concentration which secludes them from the distractions of mental busyness. In the *Way of the Bodhisattva* Shantideva describes the cultivation of concentration in relation to developing the spirit of enlightenment. It is on this that the Bodhisattva concentrates.

Chapter Six

The Treasure-trove

Geshe Langritangpa suggests another way of dealing with provocative situations that cause the disturbing emotions to arise. In our normal everyday life we cannot avoid meeting people who are very difficult. When trying to forget about ourselves and cherish others, the kind of seclusion that we must seek in such situations is not to isolate ourselves physically but to distance ourselves from self-preoccupation and self-interest.

4.   When I see ill-natured people,
      Overwhelmed by wrongdoing and pain,
      May I cherish them as something rare,
      As though I had found a treasure-trove.

When faced with ill-natured people, we should think about the fact that in the past they failed to see the harmfulness of the disturbing emotions which now overwhelm them. They became accustomed to giving them full rein and this familiarity has carried over into their present life. Nor can they have created much positive energy. All of this accounts for their unpleasant conduct.

There are so many people who are ungrateful for the kindness which others show them. Imagine you have cooked a delicious meal for a sick friend and you bring it to her. In her haste to eat she takes a big mouthful and burns her tongue. Angrily she pushes the plate away or worse still throws it on the ground. Such bad manners, so ungrateful! Our normal reaction would be to feel angered and swear never to do anything for her again. Many people indulge their disturbing emotions and do nothing to curb them. They don't see anything wrong with expressing them. It is as if they are running around stark naked, without the clothing of self-respect and decency.

There are people who commit horrifying ill-deeds, such as the five extremely grave and the five almost as grave negative actions.[87] There are others who have broken their ordination vow as a monk or nun but still shamelessly make private use of what belongs to the spiritual community. This has always been considered very wrong. In a secular context a similarly serious action would be to appropriate monetary donations or things given to an aid organization and use them for private purposes.

Then there are those suffering intensely from deforming, incurable or contagious diseases, just hearing the name of which makes us feel afraid. When we are faced with these three categories of people, we should not try to avoid or ignore them, pretend we haven't seen them or turn our backs on them. Instead of rejecting them and keeping as far away as possible out of fear or disgust, which we instinctively do, we should regard them with a sense of closeness and compassionately help them in whatever ways we can.

In the case of those who are doing wrong, we must consider what the consequences of their wrong actions will be and feel as sorry for them as we would for a man who has been condemned to death and who is being led to his execution. Concerning those who are sick, we should remember that their suffering is the consequence of past negative actions and a lack of merit. There is no knowing whether the momentum of those actions will come to an end in this life or whether they will have to endure further suffering in the future. To all of these unfortunate people we should speak kindly and compassionately and try to be helpful in stopping them from doing anything negative. If our advice falls on deaf ears, we shouldn't feel discouraged, but without harshness and without losing our kindheartedness we should continue to do what we can to prevent them causing further harm.

Others' stubbornness can be discouraging and exhausting. Our involvement with them seems to harm us and we would definitely prefer to have nothing further to do with them. The masters of this mind-training tradition urge us to avoid such thoughts at all costs, remembering how easily we could be in their place. Without being condescending, we should give practical help and in imagination take on their suffering with the wish that it should ripen on us.

People who are difficult to deal with offer us a precious chance to train ourselves to be loving, compassionate and altruistic, generous, ethical and patient. That is why they are like a precious treasure. A true practitioner feels responsible for steering them in a positive direction.

Shantideva says:

> The beggars in this world are many,
> Attackers are comparatively few.
> For as I do no harm to others,
> Those who do me injury are rare.[88]

Ill-natured and hostile people allow us to practice the patience of willingly accepting difficulties and of taking no account of those who harm us. For this reason it is right to feel delighted when we come across them and to remember their kindness since, unintentionally, they help us along the path to enlightenment.

In fact we do not meet such challenges very often. If we knew there was treasure underground or on a ship that has sunk, we would go to enormous trouble to bring it up to the surface and would certainly take great care of our find. Encountering people who challenge us in these ways is like finding such a treasure. We should be prepared to invest time and energy because through our contact with them we can increase our capacity to be compassionate. This will eventually lead us to the spirit of enlightenment and all the ensuing benefits.

If we are constantly surrounded by nice people who treat us well and by those who are in good health, we will lack the opportunity to increase our compassion. Therefore, when such a rare opportunity presents itself, we must recognize its value and cherish it. In this way we use adverse circumstances to support our spiritual practice, which is a central theme of the instructions for training the mind.

Practitioners who are already quite accomplished may well find there are relatively few people in relation to whom they can practice patience because they are less easily irritated, but most of us find that there are a lot of annoying people around. The more self-preoccupied and egocentric we are, the more enemies we think we have because anything others do that does not accord with our opinions and views is considered an act of hostility. Even a small unintentional gesture is interpreted as a snub and everything that happens is evaluated only from our narrow egocentric perspective. This can make us feel quite paranoid. One thing is certain, however: if even the great Bodhisattvas manage to find enough people who give them the opportunity to practice patience, we ourselves will certainly come across many more.

Chapter Seven

Offering the Victory

The fifth verse is about our response to those, for instance, who out of dislike and envy accuse us of misdeeds that we haven't performed. Normally, in such circumstances, we feel the need to defend ourselves, to justify what we have done and to clarify matters by either protesting our innocence or, if indeed a mistake was made, by explaining why. From a conventional point of view, this is perfectly acceptable if it is done without anger or resentment. However, the instructions for training our mind do not permit this approach.

5.   When someone out of envy does me wrong
      By insulting me and the like,
      May I accept defeat
      And offer the victory to them.

As sincere practitioners of mind training whose aim is to attain enlightenment for the sake of all living beings, we should remain gentle, calm and forbearing in the face of criticism, insults, disparagement and accusations, whether these are true or false. There is no need to embark on lengthy explanations. Simply accept defeat. Others behave harmfully because they want something; therefore we should insure that they experience satisfaction.

Geshe Langritangpa said that no matter what profound texts he read, their main message for him was that other living beings possess all good qualities and that he himself was at fault. From this point of view it makes sense to train ourselves to offer all profit, gain and victory to others and to accept all loss and defeat. Geshe Langritangpa also said that when he saw others in conflict or harming each other, he had trained himself to feel responsible for their actions.

Another Kadampa master, Geshe Shawowa,[89] said that if you think you have found anything more profound to practice in the texts, you can be sure that you have made a mistake. Geshe Chengawa commented to Geshe Shawowa that it was certainly an extraordinary practice to use adversity as something to take one further on the path and to regard all suffering and difficulty as a source of happiness.

In the *Pile of Gems Sutra*[90] the Buddha says that when ordinary practitioners who have withdrawn into seclusion to practice intensively but have not yet attained the result come across scorpions, snakes and wild animals, they should be fearless. The choice to live like this was made with the determination to give up attachment to body and possessions. Now, instead of being afraid, they should wish to help these creatures, who might even kill and devour them. They should think that ordinary gifts of food will not satisfy them and should be prepared to offer their own flesh in order to give them happiness, recognizing this as an excellent opportunity to do something meaningful and worthwhile with their body, the source of so much futility. The Buddha elaborates on this in the *Perfection of Wisdom Sutra in Eight Thousand Verses.*[91]

We practice generosity and ethical discipline to purify our wrongdoing and to accumulate merit but the purification and merit that result from offering others the victory and accepting defeat is much more powerful than that created by any other means.

If we do this, will we become weak and downtrodden? Actually the opposite will happen. Each time we are able to offer the victory to others, we grow stronger. By remaining calm and kind and by not getting angry we purify our negative actions and create merit, which ultimately is of greatest benefit to us. But it will only happen if there is no trace of self-interest in our actions. More positive energy is created by accepting others' criticism, scorn or scolding, while remembering the kindness of living beings, than by making even the most extravagant offerings.

We may wonder whether offering the victory to another person, which will give him or her temporary satisfaction, really helps that harmful person. If we are true practitioners of mind training, we bring others closer by giving them the satisfaction of being right. This can create an opportunity to help them become more mature, so that they are able to set out on the path that leads to liberation.

To offer the victory and accept defeat is a general instruction but each situation demands careful consideration. If offering the victory and giving the other person satisfaction would lead to greater harm in the long run, one should respond kindly but sternly and in that case it would be a mistake to give in. Sometimes we must do something unpleasant in order to insure long-term benefit, but if offering the victory will have helpful and constructive results both now and in the future, we should not shy away from doing so.

Someone may falsely accuse us and implicate others as well. Under such circumstances should we still offer our accuser the victory? In such a case it would probably be inappropriate since others are involved. It would be important to clear their names and establish their innocence.

The teachings tell us that we shouldn't abandon many for the sake of one but that for the sake of many, one may have to be sacrificed. This is illustrated by one of the stories of the Buddha's past lives when he was still a Bodhisattva. He was a ship's captain with many passengers on board who happened also to be Bodhisattvas. A pirate captured the ship and was going to kill all the passengers, so in order to protect them and also to protect the pirate from doing something that would bring him terrible future suffering, the captain killed him. His action was entirely virtuous because of his completely pure motivation.

This kind of conduct is risky for us because we are not yet capable of acting in a way that would normally be negative while transforming that action through the power of our motivation and inner realizations. According to the Mahayana teachings, when there is a choice between ourselves and others, we must put others first and when there is a choice between present pleasure and ultimate well-being, we must put the latter first.

In this verse the person who does us wrong is acting out of envy and the advice is to offer him or her the victory. In other contexts the advice given is that angry people should be treated with indulgence, while those who are full of desire should be treated with severity. Since envy seems to be associated with desire and attachment, should one treat an envious person in an indulgent way? Despite appearances, envy is actually more closely associated with anger. In every case we must consider what approach is most constructive. A practitioner of virtue does not respond by scolding when scolded, with anger when others are angry, by striking when others strike or by revealing another's faults when they point out his or her faults. Mahayana practitioners go further. Not only do they not retaliate, they try to help the person who is harming them by praising that person and by doing what will bring him or her happiness and satisfaction.

Our self-interest may be quite subtle and take the form of a wish for our own enlightenment, but a true Mahayana practitioner's only motivation for wanting to attain enlightenment is the wish to help others. In order to overcome self-interest to such an extent, we have to train ourselves constantly to develop sincere concern for others. If we lack sufficient compassion and love for others, self-interest predominates. When we are full of love and compassion for others, concern for them comes quite naturally. Our antipathy, hostility and anger towards others are the main obstacles to this. Since anger results from frustrated craving, getting rid of all forms of clinging attachment is essential. The more possessive and attached we feel, the stronger will be our anger when something goes wrong and we do not get what we want.

In his commentary Geshe Chekawa says that these verses are about training oneself in the patience of willingly accepting hardships, although one could also say that they are about the patience that takes no account of those who inflict harm. When we are faced with unwanted situations our normal reaction is to reject what is happening. Through this response and through the mental suffering it creates we simply add to our difficulties. Our frustration quickly leads to unhappiness, which turns to anger as soon as the slightest provocation occurs. Once we are angry, we act in ways that bring suffering. So if we get upset about small things, our reaction will create big problems for us both now and in the future. For this reason we must learn how to accept hardship with patience. This can only be done by preventing unhappiness from arising through constantly monitoring our responses.

Shantideva says:

> If there is a remedy when trouble strikes,
> What reason is there for despondency?
> And if there is no help for it,
> What use is there in being sad?[92]

Whether or not we can do something about the difficulties we are experiencing, getting upset is useless. If we can act to remedy the situation, there is no need to get upset and our energy should be directed towards doing what will change our circumstances. On the other hand, if there is nothing to be done, then getting upset and becoming unhappy won't make things better. It just increases our suffering.

A practitioner of mind training learns how to wear suffering and difficulties as an ornament, as something which increases his or her inner strength and splendor. In order to bear physical pain, sickness and other difficulties courageously, we need intelligence and the ability to reflect on the fact that since we have taken birth in cyclic existence as a result of contaminated actions instigated by the disturbing emotions, it is impossible to escape suffering in our present condition. This helps us to recognize the drawbacks of cyclic existence and arouses a wish for freedom.

Contemplating the process that keeps us in cyclic existence and recognizing how the disturbing emotions dominate us and make us act in ways that insure our misery help cut us down to size and make us feel less arrogant. These reflections remind us that unwanted suffering and pain are the result of negative actions and that the only way to avoid them is to stop acting in harmful and unwholesome ways. The happiness for which we long is the result of acting constructively and creating positive energy. Only this will lead to our well-being.

Having understood how this functions with regard to ourselves, we will recognize that others are in the same position and through this a sense of empathy will arise. They, too, are suffering in cyclic existence as a result of their actions and disturbing emotions. Empathy will lead to compassion if we see others as lovable and closely connected to us, and through this we will transcend our self-preoccupation.

With our own difficulties in mind, we can think that there are many others suffering similarly and make the wish for their suffering to ripen on us and for our own suffering to replace theirs. In this way one creates tremendous merit and uses adverse circumstances as conducive factors for one's spiritual development and as help on the path to enlightenment. Right now we may not recognize the value of these ways of coping, but when a crisis occurs and we are desperately in need of help we may remember and find them useful. This is what is meant by the inner teacher. Over the years many people have confirmed the truth of this to me.

Chapter Eight

Our Teachers

The sixth verse refers to someone whom we have helped materially or spiritually—perhaps even in both ways—and whom we might reasonably expect to be grateful. Instead they treat us roughly and unkindly. This is a situation which is very difficult to bear.

6.   Even if someone whom I have helped
      And in whom I have placed my hopes
      Does great wrong by harming me,
      May I see them as an excellent spiritual friend.

Just imagine that you have been generous and supportive to someone from another area or country. He eventually returns to his home. After some time you travel to that place, which you have never visited before, feeling confident that you have at least one friend there. Instead of welcoming you when you meet again, that person is hostile, seizes your belongings and turns you over to the police, who put you in prison. Naturally you would feel utterly betrayed by such brutal behavior, but a true practitioner sees this person who has betrayed his or her trust as a spiritual teacher—a teacher of patience.

How marvelous it would be to regard all living beings as our teachers. It seems somewhat easier to regard the harm others inflict as the result of our own past actions and to consider that they have a special karmic connection to us because of our previous actions towards them. It is much more difficult to see those who dislike and harm us as our teachers.

If in such circumstances we manage to remain kind and gentle and patiently accept these hardships without wishing to retaliate, we will be protected from a bad rebirth. The person who has behaved ungratefully has really become our teacher of patience and has provided us with this opportunity to practice. Although at present we may not even be able to imagine responding like this, true Bodhisattvas train themselves to behave in this way.

Bodhisattvas are delighted when they encounter annoying and challenging people and feel grateful for each opportunity to hone their patience. For this reason they value and respect such people. When others let us down badly and are ungrateful, we have an excellent opportunity to see clearly how far we have developed.

Bodhisattvas train themselves primarily to be loving and compassionate but for this they must also be patient. Patience cannot be cultivated towards those who help us but only towards those who are harmful. Our spiritual teacher points out the faults of anger and the great benefits of patience as well as giving us the essential instructions on how to develop patience. But we cannot cultivate patience in relation to our spiritual teacher because he or she is intent on helping us. For this we need someone who is harmful and wishes to harm us. Faced with someone like this, can we keep our temper?

Our enemies are those who dislike us and try to harm us. Doctors may cause us pain while examining us, giving injections or carrying out surgical procedures, but their intention is to help us get well. We don't view our doctor as an enemy. Although annoying people may not be well disposed towards us and have no intention of helping us, they nevertheless are doing us a favor by enabling us to increase our capacity to remain patient, and for this reason we should value and respect them.

This may seem odd, but in fact we do esteem and revere other things that have no specific intention to help us. For example, we treat volumes of the scriptures with reverence as something valuable, even though they don't have any feelings nor the intention to help us. We do it because we know that by practicing what is written in them we can develop many different kinds of good qualities.

At present we find it hard even to be patient with those who have affection for us. When out of affection and with a perfectly good intention our parents, relatives or friends give us some advice that we don't like, we quickly feel irritated. Our present love and compassion are mixed with feelings of possessiveness and attachment. What patience we have is only with those we like and not with those we dislike. We manage to be patient with important people and with those in authority, often because we have no choice and do not dare to show our anger. But when the other person is weaker than we are, we feel no compunction about expressing our anger.

The love and compassion that a Bodhisattva tries to develop embrace all living beings without any exceptions. This requires that we feel close to them all. But how can we possibly feel close to our enemies? We want to turn our backs on them and are not at all interested in relieving their suffering or helping them to find happiness. Yet unless we can love and feel compassionate towards all living beings, we will never succeed in developing the spirit of enlightenment. Despite our reluctance we must learn to relate to our enemies instead of rejecting them and this begins with the way we think. It involves trying in our thoughts to be more tolerant towards them, to understand them better, to value them and appreciate what good qualities they possess instead of overlooking them.

There are people we dislike on sight who have done nothing in particular to hurt or offend us, and others may similarly take an instant dislike to us. Those whom we dislike on sight are a special category mentioned in the instructions for training our mind. We need to take particular care of our conduct towards them. Just as someone who wants to take the layperson's vow or to become ordained or who wishes to take the Bodhisattva vow feels really delighted when he or she meets a suitably qualified person who can bestow the vow, sincere practitioners of mind training feel happy to come across those towards whom they can practice patience.

The fifth and sixth verses describe the practice of "exchanging self and others." In the fifth verse a situation is described where someone harms us maliciously. Instead of retaliating we offer all gain to the other and accept defeat. In the sixth verse someone we have helped responds with ingratitude and we accept that response, looking upon that person as our teacher. In both of these cases we are practicing the exchange of self and others by putting the other first.

When others speak to us with unpleasant words, harm us or malign us behind our backs, we should look at it as a fortunate occurrence which brings us closer to enlightenment. Bodhisattvas have particular compassion for those who harm them after receiving their help either in the form of spiritual instruction or material assistance. Instead of retaliating, all noble beings treat those who are ungrateful as their spiritual teachers and try to help them.

Our spiritual teachers are kind to us because they explain what and how to practice, and for our part we must try to implement their instructions. Similarly, difficult people act as our spiritual teachers by presenting us with a valuable opportunity, but we must avail ourselves of it and know how to make best use of it. In this way they act as our spiritual teachers. Once we can see those who would normally anger us in this light, we will not experience suffering but only well-being and happiness. With such pure perception even if everyone were to turn against us, we would not suffer.

In these verses Geshe Langritangpa singles out those towards whom it is most difficult to feel charitable. If we cannot put into practice the mind training instructions when we encounter people who call for particular patience, we will never be able to develop an unbiased attitude towards all living beings.

Chapter Nine

Giving and Taking

The instructions tell us that we should leave out none of the countless living beings but dedicate our merit to them all with a strong wish to free them from suffering and its causes. We must do this directly, in practical ways, and also indirectly, by imagining that we are doing it. We do it from the depths of our heart with no trace of condescension but with perfect respect for those we are helping. They have all been our mothers and nurtured us, so they all equally deserve our gratitude. Since they have all also been our enemies in the past, they are all equally suitable for our practice of patience.

7.   In brief, directly or indirectly,
       May I give all help and joy to my mothers,
       And may I take all their harm and pain
       Secretly upon myself.

With love and affection for them, we imagine giving them our happiness and its causes, and with strong compassion and the wish to free them we take from them their suffering and its causes. This is the essence of Mahayana practice and even though we are not yet Bodhisattvas, we can begin to train ourselves in this now.

When doing the practice of giving and taking, we imagine the living beings of the six realms of existence before us in human form. We reflect on the fact that we have taken one rebirth after another since time immemorial and all the while they have been our mothers over and over again, nourishing us with their milk and caring for us in every possible way. We have depended on them, depend on them now and will certainly depend on them in the future. Every happiness that we desire requires their help. We cannot obtain even our basic necessities—the food we eat, our clothes, the houses we live in—without them. Nor can we be generous or ethical except in relation to them. And if our ultimate goal is enlightenment, this is quite impossible without them.

Buddhas are, of course, superior to ordinary living beings with regard to their abilities and the qualities they possess, but from the point of view of our happiness we need both enlightened beings and ordinary beings equally. Buddhas come into existence because of the spirit of enlightenment they developed at the time when they became Bodhisattvas. Their precious intention to attain enlightenment could not have arisen except in relation to living beings.

Now thinking how these kind living beings lack happiness and remembering that they repeatedly experience suffering, we arouse strong love and compassion. What we visualize while doing the practice of giving and taking is not as important as the feelings we experience. There are humans and nonhumans who harm us. The nonhumans may be animals or harmful spirits. We think that while they were our mothers in the past, they did not hesitate to perform all kinds of negative actions in their anxiety to protect us. They were prepared to do anything. They had no time to develop spiritually or to train themselves in good thinking and action.

We and they have been born in cyclic existence again and again and though in the past our relationship has been close, they do not recognize us now. Because of our own previous negative actions, our presence provokes them to do us harm. They carry within them the seeds of the disturbing emotions and our presence acts as the catalyst. We are responsible for their misery because in the past caring for us kept them so busy that they had no opportunity to rid themselves of bad habits and develop their potential for good, which is why they continue to suffer. Now we provoke them to act harmfully, which insures that they will also suffer in the future. We do the practice of giving and taking with these thoughts, remembering their kindness to us.

In our contact with other living beings we should do what we can to make them happy and to relieve their suffering. If we have the will, there are so many ways in which we can help and give happiness to others. Their needs are often quite apparent if we have any sensitivity at all. The lives of those around us are full of unwanted suffering and devoid of the happiness they desire because they do not know what to avoid and what to do.

We do not feel at all inclined to help those who harm us and it is difficult to imagine helping them with any degree of sincerity. If we cannot engage with them directly, either because there is no opportunity or because it is too challenging, we can wish them freedom from suffering and the enjoyment of happiness. If even this is too difficult, we should begin simply by repeating words which express the wish that they may prosper, develop good qualities and find the lasting happiness of enlightenment. When we become thoroughly familiar with the practice of giving and taking, we can imagine taking on others' suffering as we inhale and giving away our happiness as we exhale.

The practice of giving and taking is important because all our miseries and unwanted experiences are a result of our selfishness. We imagine it as a black lump at our heart which is destroyed by the stream of others' suffering that we take on.

We can see humans and animals but there are many spirits whom we do not see. When we are experiencing obstacles, we should imagine these spirits before us and practice giving and taking. First we address them, saying: "In the past I harmed you. I ate your flesh, drank your blood and gnawed on your bones. Now do what you like with me!" If this feels too frightening, we can imagine expelling our mind in the form of the syllable *HRI*.[93] We then offer our body to them, which we imagine has become really fat and juicy. By giving them this gift their appetite is satisfied and they experience the bliss of exalted wisdom.

Having done this, we imagine that our mind in the form of the syllable *HRI* reenters our body and settles at our heart. Our body is restored, our mind is intact and no harm has befallen us. Then we should remember our spiritual teacher in the form of Amitabha on the crown of our head. He sends out a replica of himself which enters us and transforms us into Amitabha. From our heart and from the heart of Amitabha on the crown of our head, light streams out, striking the living beings before us and purifying all their wrongdoing and obstructions. They become pure and also attain the state of Amitabha.

When we finish the meditation we should rejoice in what we have done. Although it is an act of imagination, by training our mind repeatedly in this way we become more willing and prepared to do what we can for others and to act when the opportunity arises.

Chapter Ten

True Freedom

As we train ourselves in ethical discipline and in other aspects of the instructions, we will certainly make mistakes. It is therefore essential to remain vigilant and not allow wrong intentions to subvert what we do.

8. **May none of this ever be sullied**
    By thoughts of the eight worldly concerns.
    May I see all things as illusions
    And, without attachment, gain freedom from bondage.

In everything we do our guiding intention should always be others' benefit. We may be tempted to practice out of self-interest in the form of the eight worldly concerns. These are to like rewards, happiness, praise and a good reputation and to dislike their opposites—not receiving rewards, unhappiness, criticism and anything which damages our reputation. It is very easy for these concerns to tempt us to behave in ways that will attract others' approbation and appreciation in the form of rewards and respect which would enhance our reputation. However, such self-interest is utterly contradictory to the Mahayana teachings.

In other mind-training teachings this is spelled out. Kachay Penchen[94] reminds us that whenever anything good happens to us, we should imagine giving it away to all living beings as limitless as space with the wish that they might enjoy unbounded happiness. When we are having a difficult time, we should take on the suffering of all beings with the wish that the ocean of suffering might dry up for ever.

Gyelwa Yang Gönpa's[95] advice is that we shouldn't seek rewards because wealth and property add to our responsibilities and we become preoccupied with acquiring more and safeguarding what we have. To many of us the rich seem happy, but often they are greedy and discontented with what they own. Protecting what they have is a source of constant anxiety. Others envy them and they are frequently asked for donations or to support one cause or another. It seems that no matter how much people possess they always want more. For a dedicated practitioner it is much better to be poor because this frees one from a major distraction.

Yang Gönpa also says we should not hanker for praise, which quickly makes us conceited. Our arrogant behavior antagonizes others. Better to hear criticism, even though we dislike it, because it gives us a chance to recognize our shortcomings. Shantideva says:

> The rigmarole of praise and fame
> Serves not to increase merit or one's span of life,
> Bestowing neither health nor strength
> And nothing for the body's ease.[96]

There is no good reason to be attached to happiness because it frequently makes our craving, aversion, ignorance, pride and envy stronger. On the other hand suffering reminds us that it is the result of our own negative actions, and that the negative momentum set in motion by them is now coming to an end. If we are motivated by any of the worldly concerns, our practice is not pure and frustration at not getting what we want leads to angry outbursts with very negative consequences.

Kyabje Trijang Rinpoche,[97] the Junior Tutor of His Holiness the Fourteenth Dalai Lama, said that seeing the drawbacks of contaminated happiness and cultivating the ability to wear suffering and difficulties as an ornament are relevant at all levels of practice, not just in the context of these instructions for training the mind. At the initial level it is important to overcome attachment to the pleasures of this life by seeing their disadvantages. We pay particular attention to taking refuge and to the connection between actions and their effects. In the course of accumulating merit and purifying our negative actions we experience many hardships. These should be worn as an adornment.

At the intermediate level, we contemplate the fact that even the most excellent happiness of human and celestial beings is contaminated and associated with cyclic existence. For this reason it is unstable, is changeable and eventually brings suffering. We learn to regard it with as much distaste as someone with nausea regards a plateful of food. With the intention of attaining liberation from cyclic existence we train ourselves in ethical discipline, concentration and wisdom, which inevitably entails many hardships. These should be worn as an adornment, for by training ourselves like this we can stop true suffering and its sources.

As long as we remain attached to even the most trivial forms of happiness and cannot bear even small hardships, we will never be free from cyclic existence. We must also work at diminishing our preoccupation with personal happiness. Our attachment to this prevents us from developing sincere concern for others. Unless we see the faults of our present attitude, we will never be able to accomplish the purpose of the Mahayana teachings. The hardships we encounter while working selflessly for the well-being of others should be considered as an adornment.

The wish to help others, the one who has that wish and the living beings in relation to whom that wish is made are all without any inherent existence. Similarly, compassion itself, the compassionate one and those to whom compassion is extended lack any kind of true or intrinsic existence. As long as these three circles—the agent of an action, that which is acted upon and the action itself—are regarded as truly and ultimately existent, we have not understood their actual nature. Though they appear to exist inherently, they do not and are thus like dreams and illusions. By gaining the wisdom that understands their emptiness of true existence through hearing, thinking and meditating, we can free ourselves from cyclic existence. It is in relation to these three circles that we must gain this understanding and in that sense they are the basis for purification. What is to be purified is the clinging to their true existence and that which acts as the purifier is the understanding that they lack all true existence.

Our misconceptions of things as truly existent fetter us firmly to cyclic existence. The last lines of the verse express the wish for direct experience of reality, the understanding of which frees us from bondage and finally results in our attainment of the wisdom body of a fully enlightened Buddha.

The objects of our awareness, which consist of our physical environment and the living beings around us, are, like the objects that appear in a dream, lacking any true existence. We may think that at least our awareness is truly existent but it, too, is empty of such existence. Given that this is so, we may believe that the understanding of reality itself, which is the antidote to our misconceptions, must surely be truly existent. But how could it be, when neither the objects of awareness nor subjective awareness itself has any intrinsic existence, for there is nothing existent that does not fit into one or the other of these two categories. Even emptiness itself lacks any true existence, since it is also a dependent phenomenon. Thus objects, subjects and antidotes are all empty of true existence.

Between our sessions of meditation on these eight verses for training the mind, we should remind ourselves that everything merely appears to be truly existent but is actually empty of any such existence, and therefore all things are like the illusions created by a magician.

Now we return to our spiritual teacher in the form of Amitabha just above our crown. We appeal to him to bless us and all living beings to attain his state. Amitabha responds joyfully to this request and dissolves into light, which enters the crown of our head and melts into our heart. We then transform into Amitabha and from the syllable *HUNG* at our heart light rays stream out, purifying all living beings and conveying them to the state of Amitabha. This practice of imagining ourselves as enlightened beings is known as "bringing the result on to the path" and is one of the key practices of tantra.

It can be very helpful to single out the verse from Geshe Langritangpa's text which seems to be most relevant to our present situation and contemplate it over and over again until we begin to feel the effect. By doing this with all the verses one by one, each of which has inspired generations of practitioners in Tibet, and by courageously trying to put them into practice in our everyday life when we are faced with difficult circumstances, we can learn to use whatever occurs to strengthen our insight, kindheartedness and concern for others and through that also gain greater happiness, peace and contentment ourselves.

Appendix I

The Seven-part Practice from *The King of Prayers, the Prayer of Noble Conduct*

I pay homage to the exalted youthful Manjushri!

1   I pay homage with body, speech and mind
    To all Buddhas, past, present and future,
    To all those lions amongst humans, as many
    As there are in the worlds of the ten directions.

2   Through the power of this prayer of noble conduct,
    In my mind's eye I see all those Victorious Ones.
    With as many bodies as there are atoms in the worlds,
    I bow to them all, the Victorious Ones.

3   On every atom, amidst Bodhisattvas,
    Are as many Buddhas as there are atoms,
    And similarly I imagine the whole
    Sphere of phenomena filled with Buddhas.

4   With an inexhaustible ocean of praise,
    Through oceans of sound made with the organs of speech,
    I speak of the qualities of the Victorious
    And praise all those who have gone to bliss.

5   With the finest flowers and finest garlands,
     With the sweetest music, best unguents and best parasols,
     With the best butter lamps and the finest incense,
     I make offerings to all those Victorious Ones.

6   With fine clothes and the best fragrances,
     Aromatic powders heaped high as the king of mountains,
     All arranged in the most excellent fashion,
     I make offerings to those Victorious Ones.

7   I imagine giving all the Victorious Ones
     The most extensive and unsurpassable offerings.
     Through the power of faith in noble conduct
     I bow and make offerings to all Victorious Ones.

8   Whatever wrong actions I have created
     With my body, my speech and with my mind,
     Driven by desire, anger and confusion,
     Each of these I openly acknowledge.

9   I rejoice in the merit of the Victorious
     And of Bodhisattvas in the ten directions,
     Of Solitary Realizers, trainees and the perfected
     And in that of all living beings.

10   I urge those protectors who have just gained
     Buddhahood—enlightenment without obstruction,
     Who are lamps for the worlds in the ten directions,
     To turn the unsurpassable wheel of the teachings.

11   With folded hands I request those who wish
     To display the passing into parinirvana
     To remain for the benefit and joy of living beings
     For as many aeons as the worlds have atoms.

12   I dedicate the slight merit I have created
     Through reverence, offerings and confession,
     Through rejoicing, exhorting and through requesting,
     To the attainment of highest enlightenment.

Appendix II

Amitabha and the Land of Bliss

In the context of the *Eight Verses for Training the Mind* Amitabha Buddha (Sangs rgyas 'Od dpag med) is visualized in the form of an emanation body (*sprul sku*). Enlightened beings have two kinds of bodies: a truth body (*chos sku*) and form bodies (*gzugs sku*). The truth body has two aspects: the nature body (*ngo bo nyid sku*), which is the fundamental nature of omniscient mind, and omniscient mind itself, the wisdom truth body (*ye shes chos sku*). The wisdom truth body is primarily the outcome of the great store of insight (*ye shes kyi tshogs*) which Buddhas amass while they are Bodhisattvas. Only enlightened beings can perceive the wisdom truth bodies of other enlightened beings. Their form bodies are primarily the result of the great store of merit (*bsod nams kyi tshogs*), also created while they are Bodhisattvas.

Buddhas manifest two kinds of form bodies for the benefit of others. Their enjoyment body (*longs sku*) is a subtle form body which can only be perceived by exalted Bodhisattvas—those who have attained direct perception of emptiness. Such an enjoyment body gives Mahayana teachings continuously and is adorned with the thirty-two major and eighty minor marks of a fully enlightened being.

Emanation bodies appear for the benefit of ordinary beings. The supreme emanation body (*mchog gi sprul sku*), in the form of a world teacher, like the Buddha Shakyamuni, adorned with the thirty-two major and eighty minor marks, can only be seen by those with pure karma. Such an emanation body gives teachings of all kinds in accordance with the needs of ordinary beings.

Mention of pure lands (*dag zhing*) is found in Mahayana texts. They are described as places where conditions are in every way favorable to spiritual development and where one enjoys the inspiring company of spiritual teachers and supportive spiritual companions. There are pure lands from which one is once more born in cyclic existence as a result of contaminated actions underlain by disturbing emotions. In other pure lands the environment and living beings are so rich that only those who are true practitioners of the Great Vehicle and have created extraordinary merit can take birth there.

It is said that Amitabha developed the spirit of enlightenment at the same time as the Buddha Shakyamuni and others among the "thousand Buddhas of the fortunate era." Amitabha made prayers that all those who created three essential causes would be reborn directly, without having to take another rebirth first, in his pure land, the Land of Bliss (bDe ba can, Sukhāvatī in Sanskrit) when they died. For these reasons it is relatively easy for practitioners of the Buddha Shakyamuni's teachings to take rebirth in the pure land of Amitabha. It is said that anyone, whosoever they may be, can create the causes to be born there.

The first of the causes is to make or commission a painting of the Land of Bliss. Such paintings are frequently found in monasteries. One may also create or commission paintings or statues of Amitabha, make offerings before them and purify wrongdoing as well as create virtue in relation to them.

The second cause is to arouse strong faith in Amitabha and his retinue in the pure land and make heartfelt and fervent aspirations to be reborn there. The third cause is to dedicate all the virtue one creates for that purpose. Because of Amitabha's aspiration, one can feel confident that one will take rebirth in the Land of Bliss if one does these things.

The Land of Bliss lies to the west of this world, beyond many other pure lands. It is spacious and extensive and the ground is made of precious substances. Both the physical environment and the living beings in it are rich. In the middle of this pure land there is a magnificent *bodhi* tree with spreading branches and shining leaves. At its root is a jeweled throne supported by peacocks. The Buddha Amitabha sits on this throne in the vajra position. He is a brilliant and luminous ruby red. His hands are in the position of meditative equipoise and support a begging bowl full of the nectar of immortality. He wears the three yellow robes of a fully ordained monk and is adorned with the major and minor marks of a supreme emanation body. Beside him are Avalokiteshvara and Vajrapani. He is surrounded by Hearers, Solitary Realizers and ordinary beings with pure karma. All those who are with him have the five kinds of super-knowledge. In front of him is a lotus pond and from it grows a lotus which is in bud. One will be born in the Land of Bliss in this lotus when it opens.Inviting the Land of Bliss with those in it to come before us and performing the seven-part practice creates the cause for our rebirth there.

The Buddha Amitabha (Amitayus or Tshe dpag med in his enjoyment body form) is the head of the lotus family of the Victorious Ones to which Avalokiteshvara belongs. The qualities associated with this family are perfected love, compassion and the spirit of enlightenment. It is probable that this is why the Kadampa masters chose to visualize their spiritual teacher as Amitabha when meditating on the *Eight Verses for Training the Mind*, since Geshe Langritangpa's text is intended to help us develop the spirit of enlightenment through the practice of equalizing and exchanging self and others. Even if one does not succeed in doing this, visualizing Amitabha will insure a long life in which to practice and a rebirth in which one will be able to continue one's spiritual development.

Manjushri, the embodiment of enlightened wisdom, instructed Je Tsongkhapa to write a prayer of aspiration to be born in this pure land, describing to him the meaning he wished him to convey and the order in which to present it. Shortly before his death, Je Tsongkhapa presided over a large assembly of monks in Ganden Monastery and requested them to recite this aspiration (*bDe smon*) to be born in the Land of Bliss.

Also, when Jamyang Shaypa ('Jam dbyangs bzhad pa, 1648-1721), the great master of Drepung ('Bras spung) Monastery, lay dying, those around him asked in which pure land they should pray for him to be reborn and he answered that he wished to be reborn in any pure land where there were Buddhas and Bodhisattvas but particularly in the Land of Bliss.

Root Text

Eight Verses for Training the Mind
by Kadampa Geshe Langritangpa

1. May I always cherish all beings
    With the resolve to accomplish for them
    The highest good that is more precious
    Than any wish-fulfilling jewel.

2. Whenever I am in the company of others,
    May I regard myself as inferior to all
    And from the depths of my heart
    Cherish others as supreme.

3. In all my actions may I watch my mind,
    And as soon as disturbing emotions arise,
    May I forcefully stop them at once,
    Since they will hurt both me and others.

4. When I see ill-natured people,
    Overwhelmed by wrong deeds and pain,
    May I cherish them as something rare,
    As though I had found a treasure-trove.

5.   When someone out of envy does me wrong
        By insulting me and the like,
        May I accept defeat
        And offer the victory to them.

6.   Even if someone whom I have helped
        And in whom I have placed my hopes
        Does great wrong by harming me,
        May I see them as an excellent spiritual friend.

7.   In brief, directly or indirectly,
        May I give all help and joy to my mothers,
        And may I take all their harm and pain
        Secretly upon myself.

8.   May none of this ever be sullied
        By thoughts of the eight worldly concerns.
        May I see all things as illusions
        And, without attachment, gain freedom from bondage.

Notes

ABBREVIATION

P: *Tibetan Tripiṭaka* (Tokyo-Kyoto: Tibetan Tripiṭaka Research Foundation, 1956)

NOTES

1. The Mahayana or Great Vehicle (*theg pa chen po*) consists of the causal Perfection Vehicle (*rgyu pha rol tu chin pa'i theg pa*) and the resultant Secret Mantra Vehicle (*'bras bu gsang sngags kyi theg pa*). The Perfection Vehicle is the body of practices described in the Mahayana sutras by which over three incalculably long aeons a Bodhisattva creates the great stores of merit and insight necessary for enlightenment. The Secret Mantra Vehicle is the body of practices described in the tantras through which enlightenment can be attained in one short lifetime. These practices are suitable for practitioners of the very highest caliber. By virtue of simulating the desired result, enlightenment, through tantric practice, the result actually comes into being.

2. The Tibetan term *blo sbyong* is variously translated as "mental training," "mental transformation," "mind training," etc. It comprises two aspects. *sByong ba* has the sense of cleansing or purifying, and one aspect of training the mind consists of purifying negative mental habits and tendencies. *sByong ba* also means to learn or train, and

in this sense it refers to the development and strengthening of positive inner qualities. These two activities must go hand in hand.

3. The spirit of enlightenment is the altruistic intention to become enlightened for the sake of all living beings (*byang chub kyi sems*).

4. Dromtön Gyelway Jungnay ('Brom ston rGyal ba'i 'byung gnas, 1004-1064), a lay practitioner and the main Tibetan disciple of the Indian master Atisha, was the founder of the Kadampa (bKa' gdams pa) tradition. The Kadampa masters were known for their down-to-earth approach to practice, which they presented according to the three levels of capacity explained in Atisha's *Lamp for the Path to Enlightenment*. In public they laid great emphasis on the practice of sutra and kept their personal practice of tantra hidden. They regarded all of the Buddha's words (*bka'*) as actual instructions (*gdams*) for practice.

5. In 1058 Geshe Potowa (Po to ba Rin chen gsal, 1031-1105) entered Reting Monastery (Rwa sgreng), which had been founded by Dromtönpa in 1056 after Atisha's death. Geshe Potowa later became its abbot for a short time. He was mainly active in Penyul ('Phan yul) in central Tibet and is said to have had two thousand disciples. Today his best known work is the *Precious Heap of Analogies for the Teachings* (*dPe chos rin chen spungs pa*), an anthology of analogies and stories illustrating many points of the Buddha's teachings. He put this volume together because he realized that those he was instructing at times found it difficult to understand the teachings. He used analogies he had heard from his own spiritual masters, stories that he found in the sutras and whatever he heard that caught his imagination and was relevant.

6. In the *Blue Annals*, a translation of 'Gos lo tsa ba gzhon nu dpal's *Deb ter sngon po* by G. Roerich (Calcutta, 1949; reprint ed., Delhi: Motilal Banarsidass, 1976, p. 265), Jowo Lek (Jo bo legs) is mentioned as one of Dromtönpa's main disciples.

7. Atisha (known as Jo bo rje in Tibetan, 982-1054) was born into a royal family probably in what is now Bengal. Owing to his parents' opposition he had difficulty disengaging himself from royal life but eventually, after a number of attempts, he succeeded and became ordained. He studied with more than a hundred and fifty spiritual masters but was always very moved when he recalled Dharmakirti of Suvarnadvipa, the master of the Golden Isles.

Atisha made a thirteen-month sea journey to Indonesia to study with this master, with whom he remained for twelve years and to whom he attributed his development of the spirit of enlightenment. After his return to India he lived in the monastic university of Vikramashila, in what is now the Indian state of Bihar, from where he was invited to Tibet. Atisha's visit to Tibet, where he remained from 1042 until his death, had a profound influence on the course of Buddhism there. His *Lamp for the Path to Enlightenment* (*Bodhipathapradipa, Byang chub lam gyi sgron ma*, P5343, vol. 103) is the forerunner of the subsequent *lam rim* literature, which explains the stages of the path to enlightenment with strong emphasis on practice. English translation and commentary: Geshe Sonam Rinchen and Ruth Sonam, *Atisha's Lamp for the Path to Enlightenment* (Ithaca, New York: Snow Lion Publications, 1997).

8. Je Tsongkhapa (Tsong kha pa Blo bzang grags pa, 1357-1419), born in Amdo (A mdo), was a great reformer, dedicated practitioner and prolific writer. He founded Ganden Monastery (dGa' ldan rnam par rgyal ba'i gling) in 1409, the first of the monastic universities of the new Kadampa (bKa' gdams gsar ma) or Gelugpa (dGe lugs pa) tradition. His *Great Treatise on the Stages of the Path to Enlightenment* (*Lam rim chen mo*) (Ithaca, New York: Snow Lion Publications, 2000) and his other works on the stages of path were directly inspired by Atisha's *Lamp for the Path to Enlightenment*.

9. The tantra of Hevajra (Kye rdo rje) belongs to the highest (*bla med rgyud*) of the four classes of tantra (*rgyud sde bzhi*), and of the two—mother and father tantras—it is a mother tantra (*ma rgyud*). Father tantras (*pha rgyud*) are associated particularly with skillful means (*thabs*) and manifestation of the illusory body (*sgyu lus*), while mother tantras are associated with wisdom (*shes rab*) and the clear light (*'od gsal*). The Hevajra Tantra is considered of prime importance in the Sakya (Sa skya) tradition, in which it is referred to as a non-dual tantra (*gnis med kyi rgyud*), denoting that it combines inseparably skillful means and wisdom.

10. The state of Stream Enterer (*rgyun zhugs 'bras gnas*) is a stage of attainment associated with the Lesser Vehicle, whose practices lead to personal liberation from cyclic existence. There are four states of approaching (*zhugs pa*) certain fruits of practice and four states of abiding in those fruits (*'bras gnas*).

There are five factors that accord with the lowest of the three realms of existence (*tha ma'i cha mthun lnga*): the false view of the transitory collection (*'jig tshogs la lta ba*), holding misleading forms of discipline and conduct as supreme (*tshul khrims dang brtul zhugs mchog 'dzin*), desire for objects of the senses (*'dod pa la 'dun pa*), doubt (*the tshom*) and harmful thoughts (*gnod sems*). Of the three realms— the desire, form and formless realms—the desire realm is the lowest. These five factors "accord with" the desire realm because the third and the fifth prevent one from taking rebirth beyond the desire realm. While one still harbors the other three, one may take birth in one of the higher realms but must eventually be reborn in the desire realm again.

Those who are approaching the fruit of Stream Enterer are primarily engaged in freeing themselves from the three fetters: the intellectually formed false view of the transitory collection (*'jig tshogs la lta ba kun btags*) as a real "I" and "mine," holding misleading forms of discipline and conduct as supreme, and deluded doubt. The three fetters are singled out as major hindrances to the attainment of liberation. Respectively they are compared to not wanting to set out on a journey, taking a wrong road and being in doubt about what road to follow. When one has freed oneself from these fetters, one abides in the fruit of a Stream Enterer.

Practitioners who are engaged in ridding themselves of most of the above-mentioned five factors are approaching the fruit of Once Returner (*phyir 'ong zhugs pa*) and those who have succeeded in doing so abide in the fruit of Once Returner (*phyir 'ong 'bras gnas*). This means that they will take birth in the desire realm once or twice more as a result of actions underlain by disturbing attitudes and emotions.

Practitioners who are engaged in getting rid of all of these factors are approaching the fruit of Never Returner (*phyir mi 'ong zhugs pa*), while those who have succeeded abide in the fruit of Never Returner (*phyir mi 'ong 'bras gnas*) and will never again take birth in the desire realm.

There are five factors which accord with the upper realms (*gong ma'i cha mthun lnga*): desire belonging to the form and formless realms (*gzugs dang gzugs med las skyes pa'i 'dod chags*), excitement (*rgod pa*), pride (*nga rgyal*) and ignorance (*ma rigs pa*). These prevent one from going beyond the upper realms of cyclic existence. Practitioners who are endeavoring to rid themselves of these five factors are approaching the state of Foe Destroyer (*dgra bcom zhugs pa*) and those who have succeeded abide in the fruit of Foe Destroyer (*dgra bcom 'bras gnas*).

11. People are motivated by different intentions when they practice the Buddha's teachings. From a Buddhist point of view practice of the teachings is considered authentic when it is motivated at least by the wish to gain a good rebirth. A practitioner of the initial level or most limited capacity (*skye bu chung ngu*) engages in practices which make this possible. A practitioner of the intermediate level (*skye bu 'bring*) is concerned with personal liberation from all rebirth within cyclic existence as a result of actions underlain by disturbing attitudes and emotions, and engages in practices which lead to such freedom. A practitioner of the highest level or great capacity (*skye bu chen po*) is motivated by the spirit of enlightenment and does what is necessary to become a fully enlightened Buddha. Even if from the outset we are motivated by the wish to become fully enlightened in order to help others in the most effective way, we must still gain the insights associated with the initial and intermediate levels, since these insights form the foundation for the practices that are unique to the Great Vehicle.

12. The practices of giving (*sbyin pa*), ethical discipline (*tshul khrims*), patience (*bzod pa*), enthusiastic effort (*brtson 'grus*), concentration (*bsam gtan*) and wisdom (*shes rab*) become perfections and practices of Bodhisattvas when the intention underlying them is the altruistic wish to become enlightened for the sake of all living beings. The first five are said to be like a group of blind people who cannot reach the destination of enlightenment without wisdom, which is like their sighted guide. Concentration and wisdom are more easily practiced by ordained people than by lay people. Those who live the life of a householder, however, have plenty of opportunities to practice the first three perfections. Whether lay or ordained, it is important to develop enthusiastic effort, which is a delight in virtue.

13. The conventional spirit of enlightenment (*kun rdzob byang chub kyi sems*) is the consciousness accompanying the intention to become enlightened for the sake of all living beings. The ultimate spirit of enlightenment (*don dam byang chub kyi sems*) is the direct understanding of reality, namely that all phenomena are empty of inherent existence, supported by this intention.

14. The Perfection of Wisdom sutras were taught by the Buddha at Vulture's Peak outside Rajgir. As an act of homage to the teaching he was about to give he prepared his own seat. The explicit

subject-matter (*dngos don*) of these sutras consists of the stages of the profound paths of practice regarding the nature of reality, the emptiness of intrinsic existence of all phenomena, and how this understanding is used to eliminate the obstructions to liberation and to knowledge of all phenomena.

The hidden subject-matter (*sbas don*) consists of the stages of the extensive paths of practice, namely everything which constitutes the development of skillful means. Normally a hidden subject-matter is found only in the tantras, while sutras may have an explicit (*dngos don*) and implicit subject-matter (*shugs don*). The fact that the Perfection of Wisdom sutras have a hidden subject-matter places them close to the tantras regarding the subtlety of their content. They contain much that can only be understood with the help of a spiritual teacher's instructions. Of the many versions of these sutras the best known in the Tibetan canon are those consisting of a hundred thousand verses, twenty thousand verses, eight thousand verses and the *Heart Sutra* (*Bhagavatiprajñāpāramitāhṛdayasūtra, bCom ldan 'das ma shes rab kyi pha rol tu phyin pa'i snying po'i mdo*, P160, vol. 6), the most condensed Perfection of Wisdom sutra.

15. *Buddhāvataṃsakasūtra, Sangs rgyas phal po che shes bya ba shin tu rgyas pa chen po'i mdo*, P761, vols. 25-26, also known as *mDo sde phal po che*. This extensive sutra describes in detail the activities of Bodhisattvas.

16. When the Buddha Shakyamuni came to our world from the Tushita pure land (dGa' ldan yid dga' chos 'dzin), Maitreya (Byams pa) became its spiritual ruler. He will eventually manifest in this world as the next Buddha and display the deeds of a supreme emanation body (*mchog gi sprul sku*) in the role of a world teacher. It is said that if one hears and thinks about the five treatises which he revealed to Asanga, one will be reborn in the Tushita pure land. In Tibet many of the largest statues were of Maitreya, who is represented sitting on a throne with his feet on the ground, ready to rise and come into the world. Maitreya is the embodiment of enlightened love.

17. The Indian master Asanga (Thogs med), who lived in the fourth century, was a trailblazer in establishing the Chittamatra (*sems tsam pa*) system of philosophical tenets, although he himself is said to have held the more subtle Prasangika-Madhyamika (*dbu ma thal 'gyur pa*) philosophical view.

Asanga wrote five treatises on the different levels of practice. His *Hearer Stages (Śrāvakabhūmi, Nyan sa,* P5537, vol. 110), explains the paths of practice of the Lesser Vehicle. His *Bodhisattva Stages (Bodhisattvabhūmi, Byang sa,* P5538, vol. 110), which was frequently taught by the Kadampa masters, explains the paths of the Great Vehicle.

18. Manjushri ('Jam dpal dbyangs) is the manifestation of enlightened wisdom appearing in celestial form. He is represented sitting in the vajra position, brandishing a fiery sword in his right hand to denote the destruction of ignorance through the understanding of reality. In his left hand at his heart he holds the stem of a lotus on which rests a volume of the Perfection of Wisdom sutras containing instruction on the nature of reality. He and Maitreya are frequently referred to as the Buddha's foremost spiritual sons.

19. The Indian master Nagarjuna (Klu sgrub, first to second century) was the trailblazer who established the Madhyamika system of philosophical tenets which propound that while nothing has true existence, the conventional existence of actions and agents is feasible. His most famous work, the *Treatise on the Middle Way (Madhyamakaśāstra, dBu ma'i bstan bcos,* also referred to as *rTsa ba shes rab* in Tibetan, P5224, vol. 95), is a work in twenty-seven chapters which presents the explicit content of the Perfection of Wisdom sutras. It emphasizes dependent arising and explains the paths of insight related to the understanding of emptiness, employing a wide variety of approaches and lines of reasoning. This establishes it as an exclusively Mahayana text because those for whom it is particularly intended are practitioners of the Great Vehicle with sharp faculties.

20. The lineage of extensive deeds (*rgya chen spyod brgyud*), coming from Maitreya and Asanga, lays emphasis on the skillful means taught by the Buddha. The lineage of the profound view (*zab mo lta brgyud*), coming from Manjushri and Nagarjuna, mainly emphasizes the wisdom aspect of the Buddha's teachings. The inspiring practice lineage (*nyams len byin rlabs brgyud*) from the point of view of sutra starts with the Buddha Shakyamuni and comes down through Manjushri and Shantideva, and from a tantric standpoint begins with the Buddha Vajradhara and is passed down through Tilopa, Naropa and so forth.

21. The Indian master Shantideva (Zhi ba lha) lived in the monastic university of Nalanda during the eighth century. To others he appeared quite unaccomplished and they said he only knew three things: how to eat, sleep and defecate. In an attempt to humiliate him he was designated to teach before a large gathering. To everyone's amazement he showed himself to be a very great master by teaching his guide to the Bodhisattva way of life, the *Way of the Bodhisattva* (*Bodhisattvacaryāvatāra, Byang chub sems dpa'i spyod pa la 'jug pa*, P5272, vol. 99. English translations: *A Guide to the Bodhisattva's Way of Life*, Stephen Batchelor, trans. (Dharamsala: Library of Tibetan Works and Archives, 1979); *The Bodhicaryāvatāra*, Kate Crosby and Andrew Skilton, trans. (Oxford: Oxford University Press, 1995); *A Guide to the Bodhisattva Way of Life*, Vesna A. Wallace and B. Alan Wallace, trans. (Ithaca: Snow Lion Publications, 1997); *The Way of the Bodhisattva*, Padmakara Translation Group, trans. (Boston: Shambhala Publications, 1997). Verses quoted in this book are taken from the latter translation. Shantideva's other well-known work is the *Compendium of Training* (*Śikṣāsamuccaya, bSlabs pa kun las btus pa*, P5272, vol. 102), a compilation and elucidation of sutra passages about the training of Bodhisattvas.

22. Dharmakirti of Suvarnadvipa (gSer gling pa Chos kyi grags pa) was a member of the royal family during the Shailendra empire. He is known as the master of "the Golden Isles." This term was used to refer to Sumatra, Java and the islands of the eastern archipelago. The empire also included a large part of the Malay archipelago and Malay peninsula. In the Tengyur (*bsTan 'gyur*) there are six works attributed to him, of which one states that it was written in Vijayanagara of Suvarnadvipa. He passed on to Atisha the hidden meaning of the Perfection of Wisdom sutras, the extensive deeds lineage, which came down through Maitreya and Asanga as well as the lineage which came through Manjushri and Shantideva concerning the practice of equalizing and exchanging self and others. It is through the latter that Atisha developed the spirit of enlightenment.

23. A stupa (*mchod rten*) is a reliquary and usually contains relics of a great practitioner, texts and other sacred objects. Small portable stupas may be made of silver or gold and studded with precious stones. There are eight different kinds of stupas with variations in the architectural features: the Tathagata stupa (*bde gshegs mchod rten*), the enlightenment stupa (*byang chub mchod rten*), the turning of the

wheel stupa (*chos 'khor mchod rten*), the miracle stupa (*cho 'phrul mchod rten*), the descent from the gods stupa (*lha bab mchod rten*), referring to the descent from the Tushita pure land, the stupa for pacifying a schism in the spiritual community (*dbyen zlum mchod rten*), the victory stupa (*rnam rgyal mchod rten*) and the state beyond sorrow stupa (*myang 'das mchod rten*). The various parts of a stupa represent the different powers and abilities of an enlightened being's mind. On a shrine the stupa is set to the left of an image of the Buddha, which represents the body of an enlightened being, while a text is placed to the right of the image and represents enlightened speech. Stupas may also be made of masonry and may be tall buildings such as the main stupa in Bodhgaya in the Indian state of Bihar, which marks the place where the Buddha Shakyamuni attained enlightenment. All authentic stupas are filled and consecrated. Everyday implements and tools of different kinds are often placed within the base of larger stupas. These represent all the things necessary for daily life and are included to bring auspiciousness and prosperity to the area in which the stupa is being constructed.

24. Tara (sGrol ma), the embodiment of enlightened activity and the manifestation of purified energy, is mainly represented in her green and white forms. Green Tara, who swiftly comes to the rescue of those in difficulty, was Atisha's main meditational deity. From an early age he had visions of her and communicated with her directly.

25. The three Kadampa brothers (*bKa' gdams sku mched rnam gsum*) were brothers only in the spiritual sense. Regarding Geshe Potowa, see note 5. Geshe Chengawa (sPyan snga ba Tshul khrims 'bar, 1038-1103), who entered Reting Monastery in 1057, never failed to emphasize the importance of meditating on impermanence each morning to prevent the day's activities from focusing on the concerns of this life. He was Dromtönpa's attendant and taught in secrecy from his own experience to only a few disciples. He is said to have recited nine hundred million mantras of the meditational deity Achala (Mi g.yo ba), who protects from obstacles. This gave him great personal power.

Geshe Puchungwa (Phu chung ba gZhon nu rgyal mtshan, 1031-1106) was one of Atisha's disciples and is described as having acted like the man with the lump of meat. Once in a time of famine a family was on the brink of starvation and had only one piece of meat left. Had they divided it, nobody would have benefitted from the small amount of nourishment, so the father decided to eat it all to gain enough strength to go in search of food. In this way he was able to find food for his whole family. Similarly Geshe Puchungwa devoted himself tirelessly and single-pointedly to intensive practice in order to nourish others through his example.

26. The six great texts which form the basis of the Kadampa tradition are Asanga's *Bodhisattva Stages (Byang sa)*; Maitreya's *Ornament for the Mahayana Sutras (mDo sde'i rgyan); Stories of the Buddha's Past Lives (sKyes rab)* by Aryashura, *The Compendium (Tshoms),* a collection of sutra statements, as well as Shantideva's *Compendium of Training (bSlab btus)* and *The Way of the Bodhisattva (sPyod 'jug).*

27. Geshe Langritangpa (dGe bshes Glang ri thang pa rDo rje seng ge, 1054-1123).

28. Geshe Sharawa (dGe bshes Sha ra ba, 1070-1141).

29. *Byang chub lam gyi rim pa.*

30. Geshe Chekawa (dGe bshes mChad kha ba, 1101-1175) is said to have spent much time in places where the dead were dismembered (*mchad pa*) to remind himself of impermanence, which is why he became known by this name. He is the author of the *Seven Points for Training the Mind (Blo sbyong don bdun ma),* which has become one of the best-known texts of the mind training tradition. The teaching of equalizing and exchanging self and others, which is one of the main ways of developing the spirit of enlightenment for the sake of all living beings, lies at the heart of the mind training tradition. Until Geshe Chekawa wrote his *Seven Points for Training the Mind* the instructions on how to accomplish this had mainly been handed down orally to only the most promising, courageous and capable practitioners.

Geshe Chekawa gave this teaching to a group of lepers, who by practicing it were able to cure themselves. Since this was remarkable, the teaching later became known as the "leper practice" (*mdze chos*). Recognizing its great efficacy, Geshe Chekawa felt that these instructions should not be kept secret any longer and therefore wrote them down to make them more widely available.

31. Followers of the Nyingma (rNying ma) tradition primarily practice the tantras translated during the first dissemination of Buddhism in Tibet during the time of King Trisong Detsen (Chos rgyal Khri srong lde btsan, eighth to ninth century).

32. The old tantras are those translated into Tibetan before the translations made by the great translator Rinchen Zangpo (Lo chen Rin chen bzang po, 958-1055), who was ordained in 1006 and made two journeys in search of Buddhist teaching to the area loosely identified as Kashmir (Kha che) in the Indo-Iranic borderlands. He is said to have studied with seventy-five teachers during these two journeys. Later he invited a number of distinguished scholars to Tibet and translated many works with them. The later dissemination of the tantras in Tibet owed much to him.

33. It is said that the Buddha was seated at the foot of a *bodhi* tree (*Ficus religiosa*) when he became enlightened. These trees, also called *pipal* trees, are common in the Indian countryside, where stone platforms are often built around them so that people can rest in their shade.

34. Nagarjuna's *Precious Garland of Advice for the King* (*Rājaparikathā-ratnāvalī, rGyal po la gtam bya ba rin po che'i phreng ba*, P5658, vol. 129) explains both the extensive and profound paths to enlightenment, emphasizing that the root of peerless enlightenment is the combination of the spirit of enlightenment and the exalted understanding of reality. It is addressed to his royal friend, a king of the Satavahana dynasty. English translation: Jeffrey Hopkins, in *The Precious Garland and the Song of the Four Mindfulnesses*, by Nagarjuna and the Seventh Dalai Lama (New York: Harper and Row, 1975); revised in *Buddhist Advice for Living and Liberation: Nāgārjuna's Precious Garland* (Ithaca: Snow Lion Publications, 1998). In his *Way of the Bodhisattva* Shantideva expresses the same sentiment: "The pains and sorrows of all wandering beings—may they ripen wholly on myself."

35. *Lam rim bsdus don / Byang chub lam gyi rim pa'i nyams len gyi rnam gzhag mdor bsdus*, in *The Collected Works of Rje Tson-kha-pa Blo-bzan-grags-pa*, vol. *kha, thor bu*, 65b.2-68b.1 (New Delhi: Ngawang Gelek Demo, 1975). For an English translation of the verses by Ruth Sonam, see "The Abridged Stages of the Path to Enlightenment," in *Chö Yang* 7 (Sidhpur: Norbulingka Institute, 1996).

36. The two stores (*tshogs gnyis*) are the great store of merit or positive energy (*bsod nams kyi tshogs*), which is primarily created by the cultivation of skillful means through the practice of compassion, love and the spirit of enlightenment. The great store of wisdom (*ye shes kyi tshogs*) is primarily created by gaining and cultivating the understanding of how all things are empty of inherent existence.

37. Hearers (*snyan thos*) and Solitary Realizers (*rang sangs rgyas*) are intent on gaining personal liberation. They are practitioners of the Hinayana or Lesser Vehicle (*theg dman pa*), so called because their objective is limited to their own well-being. Practitioners of the Mahayana or Great Vehicle (*theg chen pa*), which consists of the Perfection Vehicle (*pha rol tu chin pa'i theg pa*) and the Secret Mantra Vehicle (*gsang sngags kyi theg pa*), aspire to attain complete enlightenment (*rdzogs pa'i byang chub*) for the sake of all beings and therefore have a much greater objective. Solitary Realizers accumulate more merit over a longer period than Hearers and do not depend upon the instructions of a spiritual teacher in their last rebirth before they attain liberation and become Foe Destroyers (*dgra bcom pa*).

38. The five kinds of higher knowledge (*mngon shes*) are knowledge of miraculous feats (*rdzu 'phrul gyi mngon shes*), the divine eye (*lha'i mig gi mngon shes*), the divine ear (*lha'i rna ba'i mngon shes*), knowledge of others' thoughts (*gzhan sems shes pa'i mngon shes*), and recollection of past lives (*gnas rjes dran gyi mngon shes*).

39. The *Twenty Verses on the Bodhisattva Vow* (*Bodhisattvasaṃvaravimśaka, Byang chub sems dpa'i sdom pa nyi shu pa*, P5582, vol. 114) explains the eighteen main and forty-six secondary transgressions of the Bodhisattva vow. For a translation see *The Bodhisattva Vow* by Geshe Sonam Rinchen and Ruth Sonam (Ithaca, New York: Snow Lion Publications, 2000).

40. The three nonvirtuous physical actions are killing (*srog gcod pa*), stealing (*ma byin par len pa*) and sexual misconduct (*'dod pas log par g.yem pa*). The four nonvirtuous verbal activities are lying (*rdzun du smra ba*), using divisive language (*phra ma*), using harsh language (*tshig rtsub*) and idle talk (*ngag kyal*). The three nonvirtuous mental activities are covetous thoughts (*brnab sems*), harmful thoughts (*gnod sems*) and wrong views (*log lta*).

41. *The Way of the Bodhisattva*, Padmakara Translation Group, trans. (Boston: Shambhala Publications, 1997), p. 53 (III. 31-32).

42. The five kinds of dregs or degeneration (*snyigs ma lnga*) are degenerate times (*dus snyigs ma*), degenerate beings (*sems can snyigs ma*), degenerated life span (*tshe snyigs ma*), degenerated disturbing emotions (*nyon mongs snyigs ma*) and degenerate views (*lta ba snyigs ma*).

43. Non-abiding nirvana (*mi gnas pa'i myang 'das*) refers to the highest state of enlightenment (*rdzogs pa'i byang chub*) in which one is free from the fears associated with both worldly existence

and personal peace (*srid zhi 'jigs pa las grol ba*). Worldly existence is compared to a sea of poison and personal peace likened to an ocean of milk.

44. The Mahayana disposition (*theg pa chen po'i rigs*) is awakened when we develop great compassion (*snying rje chen po*), the wish to free all living beings without exception from suffering. Taking heart-felt refuge again and again acts as one of the causes for the disposition to awaken.

45. The proponents of the four schools of Buddhist philosophical tenets are the Vaibhashikas (*bye brag smra ba*), the Sautrantikas (*mdo sde pa*), the Chittamatrins (*sems tsam pa*) and the Madhyamikas (*dbu ma pa*), consisting of the Svatantrikas (*rang rgyud pa*) and the Prasangikas (*thal 'gyur pa*). See Sopa and Hopkins, *Cutting Through Appearances: Practice and Theory of Tibetan Buddhism* (Ithaca: Snow Lion Publications, 1989) for a succinct presentation of these systems of thought.

46. *rang bzhin gnas rigs*

47. *zag med sems kyi nus pa*

48. *rgyas 'gyur gyi rigs*

49. The Madhyamika view (*dbu ma'i lta ba*), expounded by the Buddha in the Perfection of Wisdom sutras and elucidated by Nagarjuna, Aryadeva, Chandrakirti and their followers, is that things are neither ultimately existent nor conventionally nonexistent. Their status is between these two, in that they lack true or objective existence but exist conventionally as mere appearances and attributions made by conceptuality and language.

50. The clear light nature of the mind (*rang bzhin 'od gsal ba*) is two-fold. Conventionally the mind is clear and cognizant (*gsal zhing rig pa*). It is often compared to a clean mirror in which anything can be reflected. This emphasizes the fact that the disturbing emotions are not an integral part of it but a temporary pollutant. Ultimately the nature of the mind is clear light in that it is empty of true existence.

51. The *swastika* (*g.yung drung*) is an equilateral cross with arms bent at right angles, all in the same rotary direction, usually clockwise. It is the most widespread symbol of auspiciousness, prosperity and good fortune among Hindus, Jainas and Buddhists. This Sanskrit word means "conducive to well-being."

52. Brooms made of *kusha* grass (*rtsa ku sha, Poa cynosuroides*) are even today sold in India and are widely used. During the preparation for many empowerments, those who are to receive the empowerment are given two stems of *kusha* grass. The longer one is laid under the mattress with the tip pointing towards the head of the bed. The shorter stem is laid horizontally under the pillow. *Kusha* grass is thought to be auspicious and clean because the fronds are never tangled. It is given so that one will have clear and unconfused dreams before the empowerment and to remove anything unclean.

53. *Rtsa dur ba*, also called *rtsa ram pa*, refers to grasses such as *Agropyron repens*, which have many segments and long creeping roots.

54. Vairochana (rNam par snang mdzas) is the head of one of the five families of enlightened ones (*rgyal ba rigs lnga*). The heads of these five families—Vairochana, Ratnasambhava (Rin chen 'byung gnas), Amitabha ('Od dpag med), Amoghasiddhi (Don yod grub pa) and Akshobhya (Mi bskyod pa) are depicted making different hand gestures and in different colors associated with their particular field of activity. Respectively they represent the purification of the five aggregates (*phung po lnga*): form (*gzugs kyi phung po*), feeling (*tshor ba'i phung po*), recognition (*'du shes kyi phung po*), compositional factors (*'du byed kyi phung po*) and consciousness (*rnam shes kyi phung po*).

In this context, the position of Vairochana does not refer to the position in which he is normally shown as head of one of the five families, but to the fact that Vairochana represents the purification of the form aggregate and the *vajra* body of all enlightened beings. Adopting this position with its seven features acts as an auspicious cause for attaining such a purified form.

55. The *vajra* position (*rdo rje skyil krung*) is often referred to as the lotus position in Western literature on yoga. The right foot rests on the left thigh and the left foot rests on the right thigh.

56. This inner heat or fire (*gtum mo*) plays an important role in the completion stage practices (*rdzogs rim*) of highest yoga tantra (*rnal 'byor bla na med pa'i rgyud*). It is ignited when the energies flowing through the right (*ro ma*) and left (*rkyang ma*) energy channels are directed into the central channel (*rtsa dbu ma*). The internal fire is used to generate great bliss (*bde ba chen po*).

57. In relation to the field of accumulation (*tshogs zhing*) practitioners accumulate merit through making prostrations, offerings, requests and so forth.

58. The ten powers (*stobs bcu*) of an enlightened one are the power of knowing what is a cause and what is not a cause for a particular result (*gnas dang gnas min mkhyen pa'i stobs*); the power of knowing the maturation of actions (*las kyi rnam par smin pa mkhyen pa'i stobs*); the power of knowing different interests (*mos pa sna tshogs mkhyen pa'i stobs*); the power of knowing different dispositions (*khams sna tshogs mkhyen pa'i stobs*); the power of knowing different faculties (*dbang po sna tshogs mkhyen pa'i stobs*); the power of knowing the paths to all goals, such as what paths lead to a good rebirth, to liberation or to complete enlightenment (*thams cad du 'gro ba'i lam mkhyen pa'i stobs*); the power of knowing what kinds of meditative absorptions rid one of which disturbing emotions and the purified results they bring (*kun nas nyon mongs pa dang rnam par byang ba mkhyen pa'i stobs*); the power of knowing past lives (*sngon gyi gnas rjes su dran pa mkhyen pa'i stobs*); the power of knowing in what realm of existence death occurred and in what realm birth will occur (*'chi 'pho ba dang skye ba mkhyen pa'i stobs*); the power of knowing the end of all contamination (*zag pa zad pa mkhyen pa'i stobs*).

59. The four kinds of fearlessness (*mi 'jigs pa bzhi*) of an enlightened being are fearlessness in asserting that one has eliminated everything that must be eliminated for one's own good (*rang don du spangs pa thams cad spangs zhes dam bcas pa la mi 'jigs pa*), fearlessness in asserting that one possesses all the qualities needed for one's own good (*rang don du yon tan thams cad dang ldan zhes dam bcas pa la mi 'jigs pa*), fearlessness in asserting for the good of others what the counteractive paths are (*gzhan don du gnyen po'i lam 'di dag go dam bcas pa la mi 'jigs pa*), and fearlessness in asserting for the good of others what needs to be eliminated (*gzhan don du 'di dag spang bya yin dam bcas pa la mi 'jigs pa*).

60. The eight kinds of authority (*dbang phyug brgyad*) are authority over the body (*sku'i dbang phyug*), authority over speech (*gsung gi dbang phyug*), authority over the mind (*thugs kyi dbang phyug*), authority over enlightened activity (*'phrin las kyi dbang phyug*), authority over miraculous feats (*rdzu 'phrul gyi dbang phyug*), authority over ubiquitousness (*kun tu 'gro ba'i dbang phyug*), authority over qualities (*gnas kyi dbang phyug*), and authority over the fulfillment of wishes (*ci 'dod kyi dbang phyug*).

61. Avalokiteshvara (Chenrezig, sPyan ras gzigs, in Tibetan) embodies enlightened compassion. The most frequently depicted forms of Avalokiteshvara are the four-armed and thousand-armed forms. The latter has eleven heads: the top head is the red face of Amitabha Buddha in an emanation body form with a crown protrusion and no jewels. Below this is a fierce black face with fangs, glaring eyes and flaming tresses. Below this are three heads; the central one is red, that to its left is white and that to its right is green. Below these are three more heads which are, in the same order, green, red and white respectively. Below these are three more: white, green and red respectively. These nine heads all have peaceful eyes.

The first two hands touch at the heart with a hollow between them symbolizing the form and wisdom bodies of enlightened beings. The second right hand holds crystal prayer beads, representing skillful means. The third right hand is in the gesture of supreme giving. From it flows nectar alleviating the hunger and thirst of hungry ghosts. This gesture denotes the promise to bestow everything that is needed, and the common as well as powerful attainments. The fourth right hand holds a wheel which denotes the uninterrupted turning of the wheel of teaching for living beings.

The second left hand holds an unsullied lotus to show that Avalokiteshvara is untainted by any trace of selfishness. It also represents wisdom. The third left hand holds a water pot to symbolize the washing away of all disturbing attitudes and emotions. The fourth holds a bow and arrow to show that by teaching living beings he will lead them to the path that combines skillful means and wisdom. The other nine hundred and ninety-two arms and hands symbolize his ability to emanate universal monarchs. The eyes in the palms of the hands represent the ability to emanate the thousand Buddhas of the fortunate era. All this is for the benefit of living beings.

62. The nectar of immortality (*'chi ba med pa'i tshe'i bdud rtsi*) or the exalted wisdom nectar of immortality (*'chi ba med pa'i ye shes kyi bdud rtsi*). The Tibetan word for nectar, *bdud rtsi*, literally means "demon remedy." *rTsi* is also used to denote elixir. Like an alchemical elixir, the Buddha's precious teaching, particularly that on the nature of reality, has the power to purify demonic obstructions and to transform the base metal of our present condition into the gold of liberation and enlightenment.

63. Vajrapani (Phyag na rdo rje) is the embodiment of enlightened power. He has one head and two arms and is dark blue in color. He is adorned with jewels. His left leg is extended with his weight resting on his left foot. His right leg is slightly raised and he extends his right arm threateningly, holding a *vajra* in his right hand. A tiger skin is slung around his waist. His expression is fierce and his fiery hair and eyebrows stream upwards. He is surrounded by flames.

64. The syllables *OM* (ༀ), *AH* (ཨ), *HUNG* (ཧཱུྃ) represent enlightened body, speech and mind. They are often used to bless food when, according to tantric usage, the *HUNG* purifies all faults regarding color, taste and so forth; the *AH* turns it into the nectar of exalted wisdom, and the *OM* makes it inexhaustible. This is then offered to our spiritual teachers, enlightened beings and so forth.

65. When we visualize an enlightened being, the form we create in our imagination is called the commitment being (*dam tshig pa*). We then invoke the Buddhas and Bodhisattvas of the ten directions to come from their various abodes and enter that visualized form. They are the wisdom beings (*ye shes pa*). One of the reasons for visualizing the wisdom beings entering the commitment being in this way is to prevent us from thinking that what we have visualized is just a fabrication and not the actual being.

66. There are many versions of this seven-part practice (*yan lag bdun pa*). The words are intended to help the practitioner perform the seven activities which create positive energy and purify wrongdoing, the necessary basis for all other practices. Homage or obeisance (*phyag 'tshal ba*) is made to Buddhas, Bodhisattvas and all noble beings who are our inspiration. We then give them actual and imagined gifts (*mchod pa phul ba*), acknowledge our wrongdoing (*bshags pa phul ba*), rejoice (*rjes su yi rang ba*) in our own and others' virtue, request (*bskul ba*) the enlightened ones to teach in order to dispel the darkness of ignorance, supplicate them (*gsol ba 'debs pa*) not to pass away but to remain in the world to which they bring light, and dedicate (*bsngo ba*) our merit in general and specifically that which is created through the performance of this practice to the peace, happiness and complete enlightenment of all living beings. See Appendix I for the verses of the seven-part practice from the *King of Prayers*, also known as the *Prayer of Noble Conduct* (*Samantabhadracaryāpraṇidhānarāja, Kun tu bzang po spyod pa'i smon lam gyi rgyal po*, P716, vol. 11) is found in the tantra (*rgyud*) section

of the *bKa' 'gyur* and as part of the *Avatamsaka Sutra (mDo sde Phal po che*, P761, vols. 25-26). This long sutra describes the deeds of Bodhisattvas which the *King of Prayers* summarizes.

67. According to Mahayana teaching, no matter how negative an action is, we can cleanse and purify ourselves of it by sincerely applying the four counteractions (*gnyen po stobs bzhi*). These four consist of the power of regret for what we have done (*rnam par sun 'byin pa'i stobs*), the power of the resolve not to repeat that action (*nyes pa las slar ldog pa'i stobs*), the power of the basis (*rten gyi stobs*) and the power of counteractive behavior (*gnyen po kun tu spyod pa'i stobs*). The power of the basis involves taking heartfelt refuge and generating the spirit of enlightenment. It is so called because negative actions are either performed in relation to the Three Jewels—the Buddhas, their teaching and the spiritual community—or in relation to other living beings. We use those towards whom our negative action was directed as a basis for its purification. By taking refuge in the Three Jewels we counteract unwholesome actions performed in relation to them. By arousing the spirit of enlightenment we counteract negative actions performed in relation to other living beings. Anything positive we do with the intention of countering previous negative actions constitutes counteractive behavior.

68. In this context a *mandala* is a representation of the universe and everything precious within it offered as a gift to all those in whom one takes refuge, such as one's spiritual teachers, meditational deities, Buddhas and Bodhisattvas. The representation may be created on a round base, commonly made of copper or silver, on which heaps of rice or grain, which may be colored with a natural dye, are placed within three rings, stacked one on top of the other. As each handful of rice representing different elements of the universe is added, the appropriate words are recited. Shells, beads and semi-precious or precious stones are often mixed with the rice. However, if one does not possess such things, very simple materials may also be used, since offering the *mandala* is primarily an act of imagination. The universe can also be represented by a hand gesture which is made while reciting the verses. In certain practices one imagines the various parts of one's body becoming the different elements which make up the universe to be offered.

69. The definition of a true path is an understanding accompanied by the uncontrived wish to gain freedom from cyclic existence (*nges 'byung gi bsam pa bcos ma ma yin pas zin pa'i mkhyen pa*).

70. The union of no more learning (*mi slob pa'i zung 'jug*) refers to the union of the illusory body (*sgyu lus*) and clear light (*'od gsal*), developed through the practice of tantra and brought to perfection in the state of enlightenment.

71. *The Way of the Bodhisattva*, p. 94 (VI.112).

72. The four ways of maturing others (*bsdu ba'i dngos po bzhi*) are skillful means employed to gain others' trust and make them mentally mature and receptive to increasingly profound teachings. Since most ordinary people are attracted by material generosity, Bodhisattvas first give gifts (*sbyin pa*) and act generously towards those they intend to help in order to establish a positive relationship. When a suitable opportunity arises they teach in an informal, interesting and pleasant way adapted to the other person's capacities and inclinations (*snyan par smra ba*). They then encourage him or her to apply in practice what was explained (*don spyod pa*). At the same time, they take care to validate the advice they have given through personal example (*don mthun pa*).

73. *Chos yang dag par bstan pa'i mdo* possibly refers to *Sarvavaidalya-saṃgrahasūtra*, *rNam par 'thag pa thams cad bsdus pa'i mdo*, P893, vol. 35

74. *The Way of the Bodhisattva*, p. 94 (VI.113).

75. Ibid., p. 80 (VI.14).

76. Nagarjuna's *Letter to a Friend* (*Suhṛllekha*, *bShes pa'i spring yig*, P5682, vol. 129) is addressed to his royal friend, the same king of the Satavahana dynasty to whom his *Precious Garland of Advice for the King* is directed.

77. Pride is defined as an inflated state of mind, which arises from the false view of the transitory collection as a real "I" and "mine" (*nga dang nga'i ba 'dzin pa'i 'jig lta*) and focuses on such things as one's wealth or accomplishments. It acts as an obstacle to the development of insights and further understanding of the scriptures because it gives rise to lack of respect for good qualities and for those who possess them. It leads to a bad rebirth and to inferior social status when one is reborn as a human again.

Vasubandhu (dByig gnyen, fourth century?) mentions seven kinds of pride in his *Treasury of Knowledge* (*Abhidharmakoṣa*, *Chos mngon pa'i mdzod*, P5590, vol. 115). Pride (*nga rgyal*) is the arrogant attitude that one is better than one's inferiors. Excessive pride (*lhag pa'i nga rgyal*) is the arrogant attitude that one is better than one's equals. Overweening pride (*nga rgyal las kyang nga rgyal*) is the arrogant attitude that one excels even among the excellent or that one is better than those who are one's superiors. The pride of thinking "I" (*nga'o snyam pa'i nga rgyal*) is an arrogant concept of ego in relation to the contaminated aggregates. Pretentious pride (*mngon pa'i nga rgyal*) is the arrogant attitude that one possesses qualities which one does not possess or which overestimates the qualities one does possess. The pride of slight inferiority (*cung zad snyam pa'i nga rgyal*) is the arrogant attitude that one is only slightly inferior to those who are vastly superior to oneself. Wrongful pride (*log pa'i nga rgyal*) is the arrogant attitude that considers a fault as an accomplishment.

78. *The Way of the Bodhisattva*, p. 128 (VIII.127).

79. The ten disturbing attitudes and emotions are attachment (*'dod chags*), anger (*khong khro*), pride (*nga rgyal*), ignorance (*ma rig pa*), doubt (*the tshom*), the false view of the transitory collection (*'jig tshogs la lta ba*), extremist views (*mthar 'dzin pa'i lta ba*), belief in the supremacy of mistaken views (*lta ba mchog 'dzin*) and belief in the supremacy of misguided forms of discipline and conduct (*tshul khrims dang brtul zhugs mchog 'dzin*). In the false view of the transitory collection, transitory or perishing (*'jig*) refers to the impermanent, constantly changing and disintegrating nature of the mental and physical aggregates (*tshogs*), which constitute the basis of attribution of the person or self.

80. This division of objects is made on the basis of whether or not they are conjoined with the mindstream of a living being. When appearance, sound, smell, taste and tactile quality are features of a living being, they are referred to as internal objects because of their association with consciousness. When they are not features of a living being and therefore are not associated with consciousness, they are referred to as external objects.

81. *The Way of the Bodhisattva*, p. 58 (IV.28).

82. Ibid. (IV.33).

83. We are free from eight adverse conditions. Four of these are nonhuman states as hell-beings, animals, hungry ghosts and celestial beings with extremely long lives. The suffering of those in the bad states of rebirth is so intense that they cannot think about spiritual practice. Celestial beings with long lives are absorbed in sensual pleasures or the pleasure of concentration and cannot develop an aversion to cyclic existence. Their bodies and minds are not suitable as a basis for vows of any kind.

There are four human states which prevent authentic practice of the Buddha's teachings, the most serious of which is holding wrong views such as that there are no past and future lives and that there is no connection between actions and their effects. Being born a barbarian in a remote place where there is no access to Buddhist teachings, being born at a time when a Buddha's teachings do not exist in the world, and having defective faculties are also serious impediments.

Fortune means enjoying conducive conditions. Five kinds of such fortune are personal: being born as a human; being born in a place where the teachings exist and there are ordained men and women; possessing healthy faculties; not having created any seriously negative actions like the five extremely grave and the five almost as grave actions; and having faith in spiritual teachers, the three kinds of training and the texts which contain instructions on them. Five kinds of good fortune are circumstantial: that a Buddha has come to the world; that he has lit the lamp of the teachings; that these teachings are alive insofar as there are people who hear, think about and meditate on them; that there are those who can be looked upon as role-models because of their exemplary practice of the teachings; that support and encouragement for practitioners is available.

84. Gyelwa Gendun Drup (rGyal ba dGe 'dun grub, 1391-1474) was a disciple of Je Tsongkhapa and the founder of Tashi Lhunpo (bKra shis lhun po) Monastery, the seat of the Panchen Lamas. He was retrospectively given the title of First Dalai Lama. These lines come from a prayer he wrote called *The Eastern Snow Mountain* (*Shar gangs ri ma*), in which he expresses his devotion to Je Tsongkhapa and his teachings.

85. *The Way of the Bodhisattva*, p. 65 (V.23).

86. The twelve sources (*skye mched bcu gnyis*) are form (*gzugs*), sound (*sgra*), smell (*dri*), taste (*ro*), tangible objects (*reg bya*) and phenomena (*chos*) as well as the visual faculty (*mig gi dbang po*), the auditory faculty (*rna ba'i dbang po*), the olfactory faculty (*sna'i dbang po*), the gustatory faculty (*lce'i dbang po*), the tactile faculty (*lus kyi dbang po*) and the mental faculty (*yid kyi dbang po*). The eighteen constituents (*khams bcu brgyad*) are all of the former as well as the six kinds of consciousness which arise in dependence on them: visual consciousness (*mig gi rnam shes*), auditory consciousness (*rna ba'i rnam shes*), olfactory consciousness (*sna'i rnam*

shes), gustatory consciousness (*lce'i rnam shes*), tactile consciousness (*lus kyi rnam shes*) and mental consciousness (*yid kyi rnam shes*).

87. The five extremely grave actions (*mtshams med lnga*), which
lead straight to a bad rebirth without any intervening (*mtshams med
pa*) life, are killing one's mother, father, or a Foe Destroyer, causing
schism within the spiritual community, and drawing blood from
the body of a Buddha with the intention to harm. The five almost
as grave actions (*nye ba'i mtshams med lnga*), which also lead straight
to a bad rebirth, are incest with one's mother if she is a Foe Destroyer, murdering a Bodhisattva, murdering an exalted being of
the Lesser Vehicle, stealing what belongs to the spiritual community and destroying a monastery or reliquary monument out of
hatred.

88. *The Way of the Bodhisattva*, p. 93 (VI.106).

89. Geshe Shawowa (Sha bo sgang pa Pad ma byang chub, 1067-
1131) was a disciple of Geshe Langritangpa.

90. The *Pile of Gems Sutra* (*Ratnarāśisūtra, Rin chen phung po'i mdo*)
forms a part of the *Heap of Jewels Sutra* (*Ratnakūṭasūtra, dKon mchog
brtsegs pa'i mdo*, P760, vol. 24).

91. *Aṣṭasāhasrikāprajñāpāramitāsūtra, Shes rab kyi pha rol tu phyin pa
brgyad stong pa'i mdo*, P734, vol. 21.

92. *The Way of the Bodhisattva*, p. 79 (VI.10).

93. *HRI* (ཧྲཱི) is the seed syllable of Avalokiteshvara, the embodiment of enlightened compassion.

94. Kha che Pan chen (Shakyashribhadra, 1127-1225) was one of
the last prominent masters of the Indian monastic university of
Vikramashila. He was invited to Tibet in 1204 and played an active
role in the translation of numerous texts into Tibetan.

95. Yang Gönpa (Yang dgon pa rGyal mtshan dpal, 1213-1258) was
born into a family of Nyingma (rNying ma) practitioners, many of
whom had been highly accomplished. He displayed extraordinary
qualities such as clairvoyance from an early age.

96. *The Way of the Bodhisattva*, p. 91 (VI.90).

97. Kyabje Trijang Rinpoche (sKyabs rje Khri byang rin po che Blo
bzang ye shes, 1901-1981) belonged to the monastic university of
Ganden. He was one of the outstanding scholars of his time.

Tibetan Text
of

Eight Verses for Training the Mind

by
Kadampa Geshe Langritangpa

༄༅། བཀའ་གདམས་དགེ་བའི་བཤེས་གཉེན་པོ་ཏོ་བ་རིན་ཆེན་
རྡོ་རྗེ་ཞེ་བྲེས་མཛད་པའི་བློ་སྦྱོང་ཚིག་བཅུད་མ་བཞུགས་སོ།།

1. ༄༅། བདག་ནི་སེམས་ཅན་ཐམས་ཅད་ལ།
   ཡིད་བཞིན་ནོར་བུ་ལས་ལྷག་པའི།
   དོན་མཆོག་སྒྲུབ་པའི་བསམ་པ་ཡིས།
   རྟག་ཏུ་གཅེས་པར་འཛིན་པར་ཤོག

2. གང་དུ་སུ་དང་འགྲོགས་པའི་ཚེ།
   བདག་ཉིད་ཀུན་ལས་དམན་བལྟ་ཞིང་།
   གཞན་ལ་བསམ་པ་ཐག་པ་ཡིས།
   མཆོག་ཏུ་གཅེས་པར་འཛིན་པར་ཤོག

3. སྤྱོད་ལམ་ཀུན་ཏུ་རང་རྒྱུད་ལ།
   རྟོག་ཅིང་ཉོན་མོངས་སྐྱེས་མ་ཐག
   བདག་གཞན་མ་རུངས་བྱེད་པ་ན།
   བཙན་ཐབས་དགོང་ནས་བཟློག་པར་ཤོག

4. རང་བཞིན་ངན་པའི་སེམས་ཅན་ནི།
   སྡིག་སྡུག་དྲག་པོས་ནོན་མཐོང་ཚེ།
   རིན་ཆེན་གཏེར་དང་འཕྲད་པ་བཞིན།
   རྙེད་པར་དཀའ་བའི་གཅེན་འཛིན་ཤོག

༥ བདག་ལ་གནན་གྱིས་ཕུག་དོག་གིས། །
གཉེ་སྐྱུར་ལ་སོགས་མི་རིགས་པའི། །
ཀྱུ་ཁ་རང་གིས་ལེན་པ་དང་། །
རྒྱུ་ཁ་གནན་ལ་འབུལ་བར་ཤོག །

༦ གང་ལ་བདག་གིས་ཕན་བཏགས་པའི། །
རེ་བ་ཆེ་བ་གང་ཞིག་གིས། །
ཤིན་ཏུ་མི་རིགས་གནོད་བྱེད་ནའང་། །
བཤེས་གཉེན་དམ་པར་བལྟ་བར་ཤོག །

༧ མདོར་ན་དངོས་དང་བརྒྱུད་པ་ཡིས། །
ཕན་བདེ་མ་རྣམས་ཀུན་ལ་འབུལ། །
མ་ཡི་གནོད་དང་སྡུག་བསྔལ་ཀུན། །
གསང་བས་བདག་ལ་ལེན་པར་ཤོག །

༨ དེ་དག་ཀུན་ཀྱང་ཆོས་བརྒྱད་ཀྱི། །
རྟོག་པའི་དྲི་མས་མ་སྦགས་ཤིང་། །
ཆོས་ཀུན་སྒྱུ་མར་ཤེས་པའི་བློས། །
ཞེན་མེད་འཆིང་བ་ལས་གྲོལ་ཤོག །

Source Readings

COMMENTARIES IN TIBETAN THAT SERVED AS A BASIS FOR THIS
TEACHING

Blo sbyong tshigs rkang brgyad ma lo rgyus dang bcas pa by dGe bshes
mChad kha ba (1101-1175)

Blo sbyong tshig rkang brgyad ma'i 'grel pa don gsum rab gsal by Sha'kya
mchog ldan Dri med legs pa'i blo (1428-1507)

Theg pa chen po'i blo sbyong gyi khrid yig blo bzang dgongs rgyan
by Tse mchog gling yongs 'dzin dKa' chen Ye shes rgyal mtshan
(1713-1793)

*Blo byong thigs brgyad ma'i 'khrid yig gces 'dzin gdon 'joms byang sems
chu rgyun* by Thu'u bkan Blo bzang chos kyi nyi ma (1737-1802)